Bugging th

BUGGING
the Atlantic Salmon

MICHAEL W. BRISLAIN

GOOSE LANE

© Michael Brislain, 1995.

All rights reserved. No part of this publication may be reproduced, stored in a retrieval system or transmitted, in any form or by any means, without the prior written permission of the publisher or, in case of photocopying or other reprographic copying, a licence from the Canadian Reprography Collective.

Published by Goose Lane Editions with the assistance of the New Brunswick Department of Municipalities, Culture and Housing, and the Canada Council, 1995.

Cover photograph by Stephen Homer, 1994. Reproduced with permission of the artist.
Back cover photograph by Mark Lawlor.
Book design and maps by Brenda Berry.
Edited by Emelie Hubert and Laurel Boone.
Printed and bound in Canada by The Tribune Press Ltd.

10 9 8 7 6 5 4 3 2

Canadian Cataloguing in Publication Data
Brislain, Michael.
    Bugging the atlantic salmon
    Includes index.
    ISBN 0 86492 161 6
I. New Brunswick Guidebooks.   I. Title.
FC2467.5.T46 1994   917.15'1044   C94 950063 1
F1042.T46 1994

Goose Lane Editions
469 King Street
Fredericton, New Brunswick
Canada E3B 1E5

*This book is for my wife, Dorothy.
I hope that, in some small measure, it will repay her support,
understanding, encouragement, and above all her patience,
which has certainly been tested over the years.*

Contents

A Word from a Fish Widow 9

Foreword 13

Acknowledgements 15

CHAPTER 1
Confession & Conversion 17

CHAPTER 2
The History of the Bug 37

CHAPTER 3
The Pattern 51

CHAPTER 4
Gone Bugging 61

CHAPTER 5
A Way of Life 85

Bibliography 101

Index 103

A Word from a Fish Widow

Husband to wife: "You've been watching me for three hours. Why don't you try fishing?"

Wife: "Because I don't have the patience."

Wife to husband: "If you wanted to go fishing, why didn't you tell me?"

Husband: "Because I wanted to go fishing."

Yes, I've heard them all. It's not *easy* being a fish widow, particularly when you're a light sleeper married to a salmon fisherman who believes that unless he's up before the crack of dawn and waiting on the bank for the river to open he's not especially committed to the sport.

I have been told by sports other than my husband that he is the best fisherman on the St. John River. There is no doubt in my mind that he is. I consider such a compliment to be all-encompassing, including his proficiency in catching fish as well as his knowledge of the resource, the waters, the impact of the environment on that resource, offshore fishing, etc., etc. My husband has been studying fish since he could pick up a book and read. He has been sketching fish and wildlife since he could pick up a pencil and draw. One of his ambitions was to write a book about the friendships he's established over the years while angling for his favourite fish. I've learned to know these people by such names as Crazy Charlie, Dino, Austin, Johnny and Colin. If ever I had to reach any of these fellows, I wouldn't be able to, because I was never given any last names. Come to think of it, after all these years perhaps their spouses don't know my husband's last name, either. It's even more likely that the anglers themselves don't know each other's last names.

All fishermen exaggerate. However, there's a way to get people to believe you've really caught the trophy. One year my husband was getting ready for "The Season," and I found it somewhat ironic (brilliant, as well) that one of his purchases was an enlarging device for his camera. So often I've heard myself remark, "Oh, Michael, you're so full of it." Nonetheless, I truly believe that fishermen believe what they want you to believe.

I've never salmon fished, but for years, when we were first married, we angled for trout in Vermont. We also fished Lake Champlain at a time when anything you landed could tell you your temperature. Being young and naive, I believed it when my husband told me, "The most fish are caught on a Rapala." Early one evening while angling, I asked one sport what lure he was using.

"Red Devil," he replied.

"My husband says Rapala's the best."

"Which one of these guys is your husband?"

That's when I learned that a little knowledge can be dangerous.

Within a two-hundred-mile radius of any Orvis or L.L. Bean retail outlet, my husband suddenly comes up with a list of angling needs Saint Peter would covet. An angler's visit to L.L.

A Word from a Fish Widow

Bean is orgasmic. One afternoon we spent 65 minutes hunting down a bag of hooks — Partridge doubles. Obtaining our marriage licence and blood tests took less time.

An angler by the name of Danny (Oh, God! Now *I'm* doing it) maintains that men go fishing because of an innate desire to put food on the table. To Danny Whatever-Your-Last-Name-Is, I reply, "And Elvis was signing autographs at the mall last week."

So ends this foreword. Enjoy the book.

> Dorothy Brislain
> Fredericton, New Brunswick
> March 1995

Foreword

If you know so much about it, why don't you write a book?" Sometimes this has been said to me in earnest, at other times impatiently. I usually hear it when my preoccupation with the Atlantic salmon overwhelms general conversation at social gatherings.

I live and work in the city of Fredericton, New Brunswick. The St. John River flows past my doorstep, and a 10-minute drive will put me in the area of the river known as the Burpee Bar. A St. John tributary, the Nashwaak, flows into the river on the north side of the city. These stretches of water have served as my living laboratory over the years. It is here that I experiment and try to perfect techniques for fishing the Atlantic salmon. This opportunity to observe and fish for Atlantic salmon on a daily basis is perhaps unique in all of North America. From the beginning of the season in June through to its end in October, I can fish in all kinds of weather and water conditions, year after year — something most anglers only dream of.

From the very first day I cast a fly over a salmon in Nova Scotia in 1973, I have kept a diary. What prompted me to do so, I don't quite know. Perhaps it was a notion that in the future the collected information would be useful. For four years, these diaries consisted mainly of details about the autumn salmon runs of the Bay of Fundy's Minas Basin.

I continued my diaries when I started fishing the rivers of New Brunswick in 1977. My notes contain a rich diversity of information: fish raised, taken, released or lost; what fly I used; weather and water conditions as they changed over the seasons; the insect and other life which abounds along the rivers; the changes in the rivers themselves; and the political and management issues relating to the fish stocks. Just about everything that is of importance to a dedicated salmon angler can be found in my little books.

During the winter of 1994 I found myself going over diary entries dating back to the very beginning of my involvement with the Atlantic salmon on the St. John River and thinking that perhaps I could do something with them. The decision to write this book was the result of such perusals. My goal is not so much to produce a definitive work of salmon fishing as to simply share with you my own experience of fishing the Atlantic salmon with a bug. If after reading this material you are prompted to experiment with tactics, or if you have garnered some new information that you may put to use, then my effort has been worthwhile.

Acknowledgements

I wish to acknowledge the debt I owe to my father, Lorne Brislain, and my great-uncle, Cedric Patton; childhood memories of our Sunday outings on Alder Brook will be cherished always.

I would like to express my gratitude to Roy Seaman, my ninth-grade teacher; to my friend, Dr. Danny Bate-Boerop, whose counsel I will always value; to Emelie Hubert, whose editorial expertise and suggestions for this book were invaluable; and to all my fellow anglers whom I've had the pleasure to know, however briefly, over the years.

With all salmon anglers, I owe a debt of gratitude to the Atlantic Salmon Federation. This voluntary non-profit organization depends on the support of anglers and conservationists in its world-wide efforts to save and enhance Atlantic salmon stocks. Its address is PO Box 429, St. Andrews NB Canada E0G 2X0.

CHAPTER 1

Confession & Conversion

If I have learned anything over the years about the Atlantic salmon, it's that it is an unpredictable fish. For instance, everyone knows that Atlantic salmon do not feed in fresh water during their spawning run, yet I have a first-hand report of a June fish of some 10 pounds that was stuffed with forest tent caterpillars. This occurred in 1981, when the heavy infestation of tent caterpillars defoliated large tracts of hardwood and created a road hazard because their squashed bodies made the highways very slippery.

    Constants are few. There are not many guidelines which will enable one to develop the tactics that allow the angler to achieve even a modicum of success, and just when you think you have resolved a particular angling problem a new one replaces it. In 1979 I failed to land a single salmon after putting in some hundred hours of angling time on one particular river. The autumn wet fly tactics and patterns I was accustomed to were not working on New Brunswick's summer waters. Then, a few years ago, for a stretch of two weeks beginning in July, the majority of the fish taken succumbed to a simple, nonde-

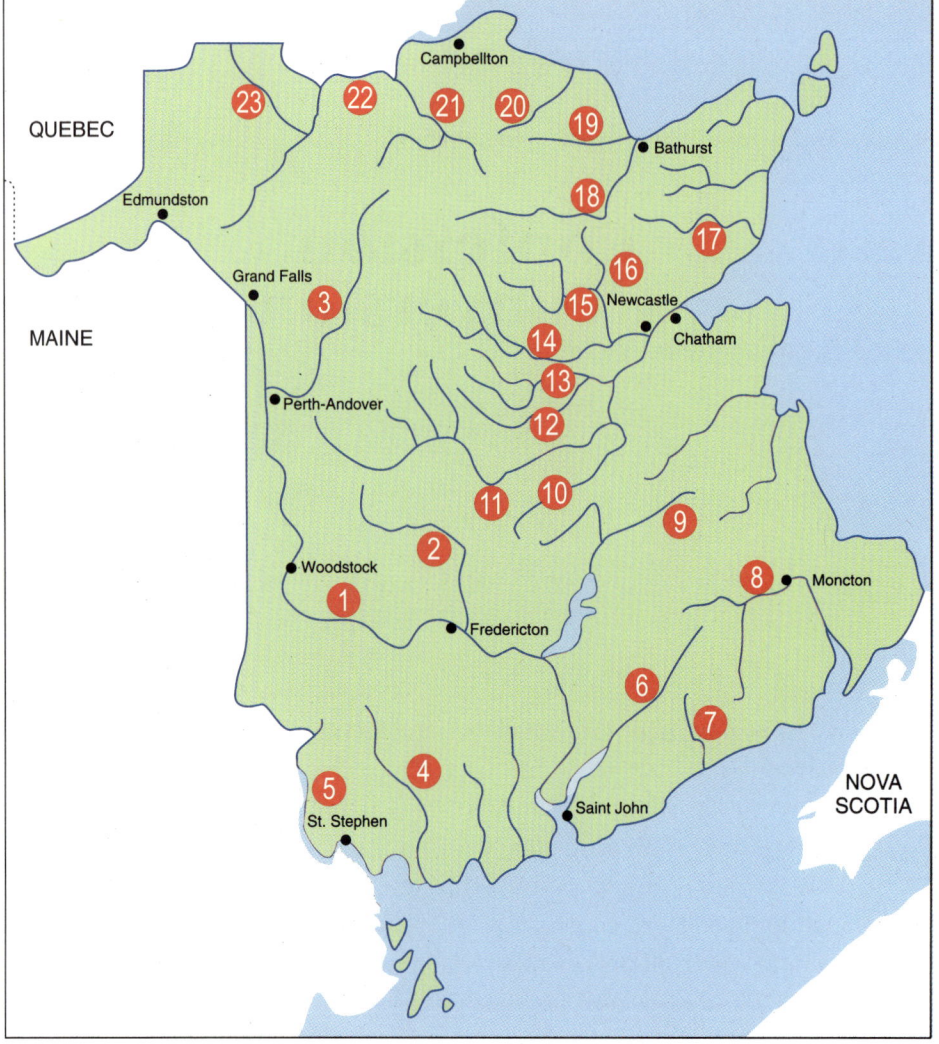

Major Salmon Rivers of New Brunswick

1. St. John River
2. Nashwaak River
3. Tobique River
4. Magaguadavic River
5. St. Croix River
6. Kennebecasis River
7. Big Salmon River
8. Petitcodiac River
9. Salmon River
10. Cains River
11. Main Southwest Miramichi
12. Dungarvon River
13. Renous River
14. Little Southwest Miramichi River
15. Sevogle River
16. Northwest Miramichi River
17. Tabusintac River
18. Nepisiguit River
19. Tetagouche River
20. Jacquet River
21. Upsalquitch River
22. Restigouche River
23. Kedgwick River

script wet fly, a #4 silver-bodied black bear hair pattern, with a sparse black hackle.

Over time, I have graduated from being a *tourist* on the St. John River to the status of a *regular*. To be a regular, you have to be prepared to be up in time to start fishing the runs at 4:45 AM. At 7:30, it's time to quit, drive home, change clothes, and put in a full day's work. I've grown accustomed to this routine over the seasons, or have convinced myself that I have. In 1982, five years after starting to fish here, I became dimly aware that certain of my fellows were enjoying considerable success while I could only shake my head in consternation.

One August day before dawn, my friend Harold pulled out his fly box and handed me a #6 Mustad Bronzed Double Red Butt Buck Bug. "I know you don't think much of them, Mike," he said, "but I've taken home two salmon and six grilse on this thing so far this year, and I'm not counting how many fish I've raised or lost."

I accepted the pattern and used it infrequently that year without success. I put it aside. During that and subsequent seasons, I did take an occasional fish on the bug but dismissed the event as being of little consequence. I attributed it all to the fish wanting something different.

Harold was right; I didn't think much of the bug.

My first introduction to it had been far from favourable. The year was 1981, and for three glorious days in August I was going to fish at the provincial government camp known as Larry's Gulch. It lies in a sunken valley just below the confluence of the fabled Kedgwick and Restigouche rivers. The lease varies from swiftly flowing runs merging with deep holding water to slick glides, with cliffs that rise almost vertically. Tinged an emerald green, the water has incredible clarity. You can see an individual pebble 20 feet down.

We arrived at the camp at about 6:00 PM and were too excited to notice the dour mood of the guides. The river was

19

low, and the fish's temperament matched the conditions. We had just missed dinner and Jimmy, the camp manager, was in the process of organizing the evening fish. Drawing a slip of paper from the old battered felt hat, I was pleased to see that Charlie would be my guide that evening and for the next three days.

Jimmy, always the gracious host, handed me a ham and cheese sandwich and a thermos of tea as I hurried down the steep gravel path to the river, where Charlie sat waiting in the canoe. I barely had time to get settled in before Charlie raised anchor, letting the 16-foot Chestnut swing into the main current. He cranked up the Evinrude, and with a muffled sputter the engine came to life, planing the canoe swiftly up river.

Now, Charlie was nearly seventy at the time. He informed me matter-of-factly that this was probably his last year of guiding. From the old school, he maintained an attitude of caution and restraint towards people he did not know, perhaps the best policy for a man who guides for a living. After talking with Charlie for a while, I deduced that not all anglers dealt with their guides as equals, that too often sports were opinionated and looked upon guides as the hired help.

We anchored in the run of the Fence Pool. I was tired after the long drive from Fredericton, and I was content just to be out on the river. The stillness in the gorge was calming. I would be earnest tomorrow. Here, in this place that time had changed so little, I was lost in my own thoughts. Pointing out an old caribou trail on the far shore, Charlie brought me back to reality. It had been fifty years since caribou had lived in this area, although every few years someone would report a sighting. If it was not a mistaken identification, it was most likely a stray; further north, a small herd of about three hundred or so lies hidden in the deep defiles of the Gaspé's Chic Choc Mountains. The old trail was still clearly visible in the foot-deep moss of the forest floor as it wound its way through the spindly black spruce towards the summit of the rim. Trails such as this are all that remain of the thousands of woodland caribou that once roamed the wilderness of northern Maine and New Brunswick.

Charlie talked on. "It was six years ago now, and this young fella come from Nova Scotia, carrying God knows what in the way of tackle. He had money all right. I could tell that when I seen his big white Seville parked beside the main lodge. He was talking to Jimmy as I walked down from the guide shack. He was agoing on about having to share a room, and he wasn't too happy about it, having quite a chaw, he was. Jimmy explained things, like that he was lucky to have water, especially being from out of province. The only reason he got to fish was because someone had cancelled out and he knew some of the bigshots in Freck'ton.

"Jean was a big St. John River Frenchman from Madawaska, Maine, just across the line. He owned timber leases in the province. He liked to come to the Gulch, relax, drink a few quarts of rye, and let the guide do the fishing. [This is against the law now, but it wasn't then.] He made his money in lumber, with his wits and his fists. I guess you'd call him a lumber baron, something like Irving in these parts. I darest say Jean never got past the third grade, but some sharp.

"I was at loose ends, so I decided to stick around, out of the way mind you, but close enough to see what was going to happen. I looked inside the unit. Jean was lying on his bed with just his pants on, and those big striped suspenders adangling. In one hand he had a book of sorts and in the other a quart of Canadian Club.

"Well, this new fella was giving Jimmy every bit of a hard time, all the while laying his gear out on the bed. There was a bamboo salmon rod, graphite and glass rods. Boxes and boxes of flies, five or six reels, must have been custom made. Floating lines and sinking lines. You name it. If it was made for salmon fishing, he had it.

"All the while, Jean just lay there not saying a word, just taking it all in. When he did raise his eyes up over the book, you could tell he wasn't getting real enthusiastic about his new roommate. Quick as a cat, he was on his feet. It was sort of amazing for the big man that he was, well over six foot and not a pound under 300.

"He stood there behind Jimmy and this sport to look a little more closely at the goings on. This fella was still telling Jimmy how and what he should do, all the while telling him how fine and expensive his gear was, and that he expected his limit. Jimmy was a bit startled when he turned around and saw Jean towering over his left shoulder, and he says to him, 'Jean, this is Bernard, he's come in from Nova Scotia and he'll be sharing . . .'

"Jimmy didn't get to finish the sentence. In his great deep gravelly voice, Jean says, 'Look at all dat goddam shit.' He didn't say another word, and he crashed back onto the bed with his book. You could have heard a pin drop. I thought Jimmy would bust out laughing. He was having one hell of a time trying to keep a straight face."

Charlie and I were both laughing at the end of his story. Charlie had a true appreciation of human nature in all its forms. He reminded me of my great-uncle Ced, who had that same halting chuckle. It came from the heart and held the wisdom of age.

"Well, we still have a couple of hours before it gets too dark, so you might as well get started. It was here yesterday a fella took a forty-three-pound fish on a Johnny Bug. Set a new camp record."

I showed Charlie what I had in my fly box. He politely fingered a few and selected a small #10 Brown Fairy, which

Confession & Conversion

Anglers on the Nashwaak. ATLANTIC SALMON FEDERATION

quite surprised me. If anything, I would have selected a #4 or even a #2.

"You might want to try this one, the water is low now and the fish are taking soft. Just throw it out a ways, not too far."

Tentatively, I began to cast. Charlie sat in the stern watching intently, smoking his Export Plains. God, I thought, one drag on that cigarette would be enough to floor me! After a while he motioned me to reel in and we drifted down another 10 feet before we dropped anchor. The sun was getting low, reflecting a deep tranquillity against a wall of black spruce.

"Here, try this."

Before I could say another word, he had knotted a white bug with an orange hackle and a fluorescent butt of the same colour. I was not unfamiliar with the pattern and naturally assumed he would also dope it up so I could fish it as a dry fly. But no, he proceeded to mash the fly into the discoloured water that had collected between the ribs of the canoe, squeezing out as much of the entrapped air as possible. He said, "Drop it over there, and let it drift just under. Try to keep the drag down. If it skims, draw the fly towards you, then drop your tip."

On the fourth drift the river opened up. A huge salmon breached beside the fly. I reacted by pulling up short. I should have waited.

"Aw, damn," Charlie exclaimed, as he rose in the stern, pointing. "Twenty-five pounds at least. You didn't prick him, I think he'll come back."

Half an hour later, after using different patterns among frequent rests, nothing had happened. I put the bug back on again. On the first drift the fish appeared out of nowhere. I had a brief glimpse of the broad back as the salmon turned down. Trying to raise the rod and take up the slack at the same time, I was caught off balance. I could feel the weight, the hook attempting to get a bite. Then slackness in the line and the receding rings of the rise gently lapping the side of the canoe. I just stared, open-mouthed. It took me a minute to regain my composure.

The shadows were lengthening. Little brown bats flitted low in the gathering darkness. We pulled anchor and drifted lazily down to the bogan below the Fence Pool. Charlie set the pole and pointed toward the shallows. At first I did not see what I was looking at, but slowly the realization set in. The bottom was moving. The bottom was not the bottom at all, but literally a mass of salmon. "I figure there's close to a thousand

Confession & Conversion

fish lying in here," Charlie said. "I've seen a couple that would go over fifty."

I had never seen such a sight before, nor will I probably ever see it again.

I was up the next morning at six, an hour or so before breakfast. I went into the kitchen to get a cup of tea and meet Charlie. At this hour, dawn was breaking. We sat outside in the cool dampness of the early morning. The landscape was like a surrealist painting, with an eerie sun shining through the heavy mists steaming off the river.

Charlie told me that I had come at a bad time. The fish were there, but only a few were being taken, mostly on bugs. I regret to say that I was sceptical. Surely a dry fly or a small wet would produce some fish, I told him. He just smiled. Unfortunately for me, my views at the time were strongly prejudiced in favour of conventional flies and tactics.

Charlie commented on the rod I was using. I told him it was a Graphite 9 1/2' Tournament Tarpon Rod that would drive an 11-weight line clear into the backing. "It's a nice rod, okay for fishing #2 doubles or 1/0's in June and July, but sort of heavy for fishing bugs. Perhaps you might want to use this one." He offered me a 9' glass Hardy, matched with an 8-weight line. I politely declined his offer. I was bound and determined to catch a salmon on *my* terms, with *my* flies and *my* equipment.

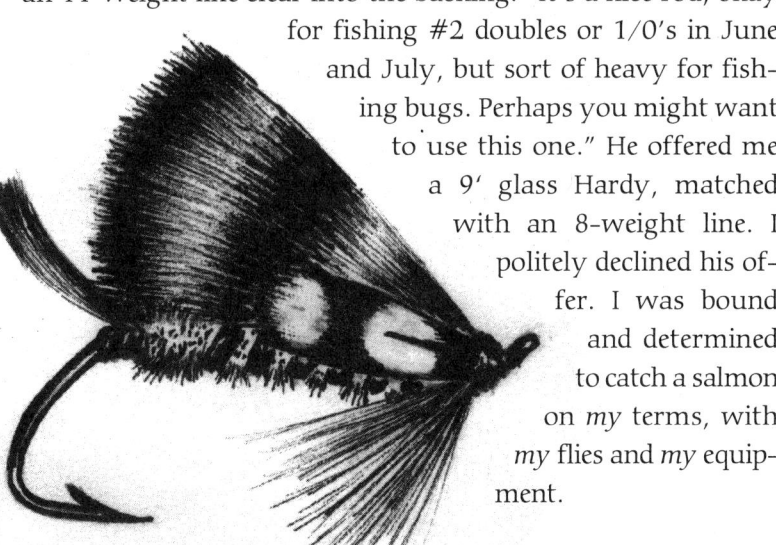

Brown Fairy

Bugging the Atlantic Salmon

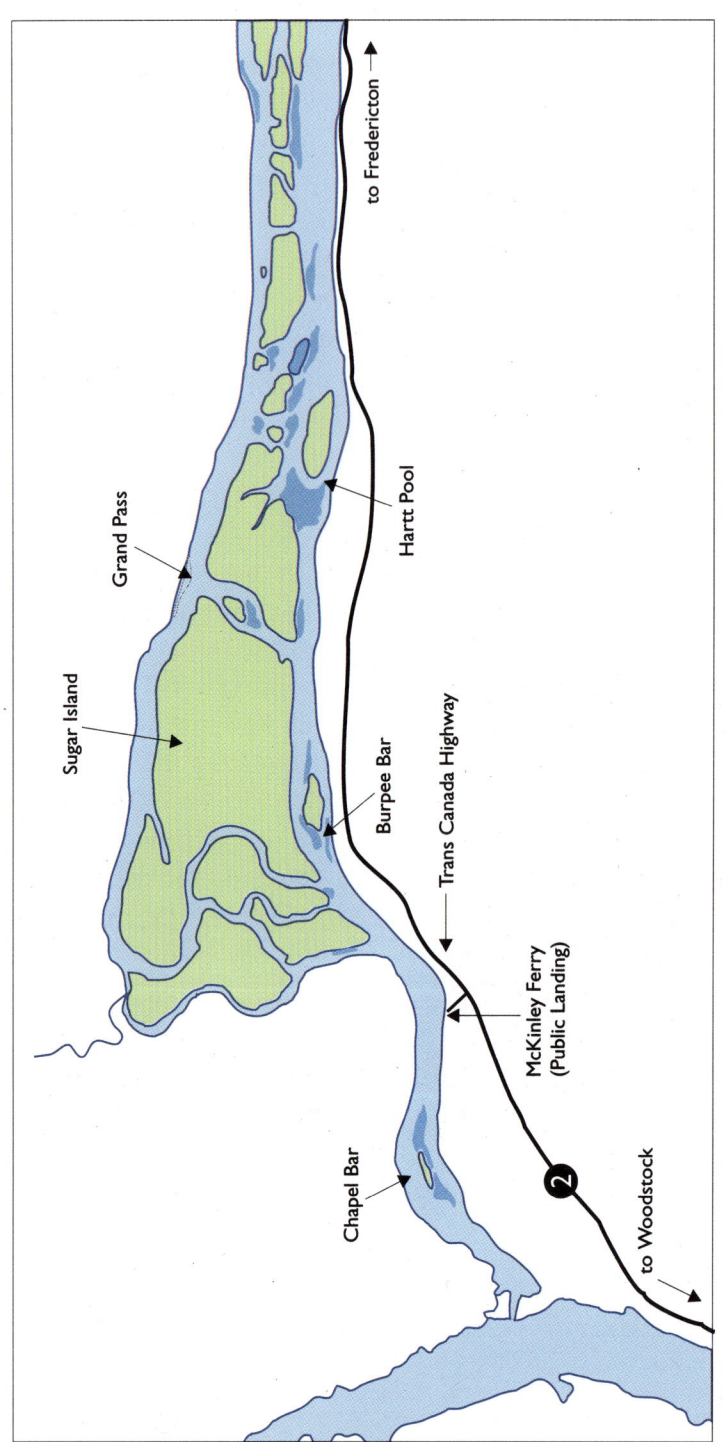

The Burpee Bar near Fredericton, New Brunswick

Confession & Conversion

For the next two days, I filled the air with dry flies and small wets, drifted, skittered and stripped in with hand-twist retrieves that produced four rises. I used bugs only occasionally, more to satisfy Charlie than because of any belief I had in their worth. Of the eight salmon landed at the camp by other anglers, six had succumbed to bug patterns, the largest being a 26-pound fish. But I attributed it all to luck, going home with just memories and without my brace of 20-pounders. There was, however, a nagging feeling in the back of my mind that I should have paid attention. When I read through the notes I had made of that excursion, I realized that I had become intransigent, a victim of tradition.

To this day, the Restigouche, one of the greatest salmon rivers of the world, remains tradition-bound in many ways, and Charlie was born and raised there. Yet when he was nearly seventy years old he taught me an important lesson: never be afraid to try something new, and don't be in too much of a hurry to dismiss it lightly.

Even so, it was not until 1989 that I began to weave events, tactics and observations into a comprehensive procedure. I have my opinions as to why salmon will rise to a fly, though the issue will remain as contentious in angling circles in the future as it has done in the past. But I now believe fishing with a bug to be one of the best methods of fly fishing for Atlantic salmon, outproducing the traditional wet- and dry-fly tactics which have become enshrined and are viewed by many as gospel.

August 3, 1986. I had risen early, at about 4:30 AM. On the horizon, a faint pink band was etched against an inky black sky. The stars, sparkling points of diamond-white light, seemed close enough to touch. All was quiet in the coolness of the hour. It was still a little too early in the season for crickets, but the fireflies were still active, trailing winking green fluorescent wakes as they sailed by. Only an occasional robin called at that hour. I sat outside on the deck with a mug of hot sweetened tea to contemplate the challenges of the day.

According to the reports I had been receiving, there was a good run of grilse moving up the St. John. Many of the fish that had been taken were "just legals," close to the 25" limit and weighing six to eight pounds. On some other rivers, these large grilse would be classed as salmon, but not on the St. John. I suspect that they are endemic to a particular watershed further upstream, more than likely a tributary of the Tobique. Two days before, a friend who had had little exposure to salmon fishing used a bug in the runs. He hooked three fish and landed two grilse. Of all the anglers there, he was the most successful one that morning.

I looked at my watch; it was time to get on the road. A leisurely 10-minute drive upriver brought me to the Burpee Bar. As always, it was a challenge to pick my way along the path and the faint trail in the broken ledge that lined the riverbank, especially so when the moon was down. For the life of me, after all these years, I still won't use a flashlight, even though the riverbank can be treacherous, damaging to both the angler and his equipment. I slipped and broke my leg on one occasion. Luckily, it was at the season's end.

When I arrived at the head of the run, Dino, Harold and Austin were there, their low conversation muffled by the rush of falling water. A half hour before sunup, out came our penlights, accompanied by the opening snap of our various fly boxes.

"Now there's one, Harold," said Dino. "You see that? That's tied with a tail of white rabbit fur instead of a fluorescent butt, and it's smaller, a #8. It has a lot more action and will be more effective."

"Well, be that as it may, I'm still going to use this Green Machine," said Harold, sceptical of the proffered fly.

"Mike's not saying too much this morning," chided Austin. "He must be going to use that Brown Fairy again."

"No, I think perhaps I'll try a bug."

"You'll try a bug?" chirped Harold. "I thought you didn't believe in them."

"Well, I don't, really, but I think they have their worth from August onwards when the water warms." Until then I had never made a conscious effort to fish bugs, but I was beginning to become aware that they were something much more than just a simple deer hair pattern.

My attention was diverted by the discussion between Doc and Austin. You had to know Doc to appreciate his dry sense of humour. He was a product of the old colonial system — someone said that he had grown up in Hong Kong, complete with an amah. He spoke succinctly, with a clipped British accent diminished only somewhat by his years in Canada. When the occasion merited, he would use the inflection in his voice to signal a put-on that would double us up with laughter.

Austin shone his penlight down the rows of his Wheatley fly box, exposing row after row of exquisitely crafted wet flies. He stopped at a bedraggled #6 Red Butt Bug. Dead serious in his dissertation on the fly, he said. "And this bug is *the* most productive fly this year."

Ever so slowly, Doc picked up the bug, turning it around and over as he held it up to the faint dawn light.

"Bit of a peasant's fly, what!"

Austin, after a moment's hesitation, roared with laughter, calling Doc between fits of hilarity an arrogant limey son of a bitch.

Bugging the Atlantic Salmon

Angling on the Burpee Bar. ATLANTIC SALMON FEDERATION

We played our ritual game of one-upmanship, sometimes jokingly, at other times in a quite serious vein. There is a magic in the still predawn that draws together a diversity of men to share a common bond. Our discussions were eclectic, ranging from the cost of this year's car insurance to the composition of interstellar matter. Usually about this time Crazy Charlie would motor down to fish the other side of the run. How he could navigate at full throttle, even on dark stormy mornings, without piling the boat up on the bar never ceased to amaze us.

At precisely 5:25 Harold announced that it was time to begin. It was his way of saying that daylight was cracking over the low ridges, signalling his impatience to fish. While the others used their penlights to assist them in tying fly to leader, I did it the old-fashioned way, my fly and leader silhouetted in the faint light.

Confession & Conversion

Dawn on the Burpee Bar. MARK LAWLOR

We began by taking up position, spread out along the upper bar. In the early morning, fish would be resting anywhere up- and downstream from the huge boulder that lies exposed when power generation isn't taking place at the Mactaquac Dam upstream. Occasionally we could see salmon slipping up over the bar in the half-light.

Downstream from this boulder lies a 500-yard stretch of broken water that deepens as it tumbles downstream. On the other side of this run, a gravel bar parallels the riverbank for some three-quarters of a mile. Another channel separates this bar from Sugar Island, which lies about half a mile further out from where we were now standing. This whole area of the St. John is interlaced with numerous runs, bars, channels and pools; it could easily accommodate hundreds of anglers fishing from boats.

At the head of the run, water piles up against a large, submerged, shelved-up ledge. Just over to one side, where the water ripples and eddies, a salmon is usually lying early in the morning. As usual, Harold was the first to hook a fish. Through the light mist, I could see him, rod held high as he followed the running fish downstream. On the other side of the point, where the broken water ends, I caught a glimpse of a jumping grilse as it flashed against the rising sun. Shortly after, Harold beached his fish and knelt on the hard shale to tag it.

I was starting to enter the head of the run when he walked by and showed me his catch. It was a fresh fish, black of back, with that characteristic purple tinge to the silvery sides. It would probably go about six pounds, a grilse with the proportions of a salmon.

"Harold, I suppose you got him on a bug?"

"No, took him on a Conrad. You might want to fish that Brown Fairy of yours in the run, but once you get down past the point use a Green Machine in the slower water."

"Good advice. I'll keep it in mind if I don't have any takes in the run."

Austin and Dino had preceded me past the lie where Harold had hooked his fish. Usually the area holds more than one. Sure enough, as my #8 Brown Fairy swung it was met with a flurry as a grilse ploughed into the fly. Just as quickly the fish was gone.

I continued down the run for about an hour or so. Dino and Austin hauled out at the point and prepared to walk back up to the head of the bar to fish it through again. On reaching the same spot a little later, I reeled in. Sitting down on the broken spine of ledge that formed the point, I thought about changing the fly. My fingers ran down the rows of patterns and stopped at a bug, a little #8 Green Machine with a red and green fluorescent butt. I had tied a few up earlier in March, merely as an exercise and a change of pace.

Well, I thought, Harold said to use them in the slower water. Since I had the time this morning, why not? I proceeded down the run to where the current slowed and eddied as it dumped into the broadening channel. The area, known as the Glory Hole, had in the past produced some outstanding fish, but in June, at the beginning of the season, when the water was considerably cooler. It was common knowledge that fish held here all season long, the consensus being that a number of cold springs well up from the bottom. Adjacent to the run a steep bank rose some sixty feet or more, and on it there were tangled alders to snag any low backcast. Now, with the season getting on and the water warming, few anglers ventured down this far. The rewards of fishing this section were not considered to be worth the effort, yet everyone was aware that, though the popular upper run might be devoid of fish, you could nearly always spot one rolling down in the Glory Hole.

The sun was well up by eight o'clock, masked now and then by banks of broken cloud scudding slowly with the prevailing westerlies. The river surface was still, mirroring the oily reflections of cloud and sky. Only the occasional parr interrupted the calm, dimpling, minute Caenis spinners. Their flights are common on such warm August mornings; in spite of the destruction man has wrought, the river still holds a rich diversity of life. The sharp, rapid, whistling "chip-chip-chip-chip" of an osprey brought me out of my reverie. From the corner of my eye, I spotted the almost imperceptible head and tail rise of a salmon. I knew from long experience that this fish was hanging above a tabletop jumble of ledge that came within four feet of the surface. Further downstream there were similar outcroppings of the river bottom over which fish would hold.

I worked down towards the fish, casting the bug randomly until I was about twenty feet or so above the lie. I had seen Harold on more than one occasion work a bug through the Glory Hole with impressive results. I had always noted that he never cast downstream; rather, he turned so that he was able to cast across. His fly would then drift at least three or four feet before it passed over the lie.

I did my best to place the cast up and across, finding this easier to accomplish when I shortened the line. The bug was dropped precisely and allowed to drift, the current flow was even, and mending was not required. I continued the step-and-cast rhythm, all the while carefully and quietly working myself into position.

Ten feet above the lie I reeled in to check the bug. With so much broken ledge lining the bank, it was all too easy to bang the barb off the fly. You would never discover the loss until that salmon shook loose and you wondered why.

Laying a cast directly downstream to extend the line, I lifted and rotated the pickup. The bug landed upstream from the lie. It had drifted about four feet or so when I noted the classic humping of the water. I waited, resisting the urge to pull. The bug continued its drift. Just before the cast was fished out, I saw the telltale wake curving in. The salmon took the bug as it turned. A swirl, a tug, and I lifted sharply, feeling the weight. For a moment, the rod stood out, bowed, line thrumming in the slight flow. As is usual with slow starters, the fish began with savage head shaking. I could feel the thump vibrating down the rod each time the fish whipped from side to side. I waited. Slowly, the bow of the rod became more pronounced as the strain increased. "Whaaaaaaa," screamed the reel as a dozen feet of line ripped away in an instant. Seconds later the big grilse bounced skyward. He was off and running the moment he touched down, exploding with the razzle-dazzle that only a grilse is capable of. I got the fish turned after the second run, gradually edging him into the shallows. Just as I reached down to tail him, he was off like a shot, throwing water everywhere. With the bucking rod in one hand, I got my glasses off and fumbled them away into my vest. The fish was out a little way, putting his broad side to the current, levering against the pull of the rod. Harold had walked down from the point to get a better look at the proceedings, and it was just now that I noticed him behind me.

"This is one strong fish. I think he's a little too big."

"Nah," said Harold. "He's a good fish, I got a pretty good look at him on that last jump. He'll make the limit. What did he take, a bug?"

"Yes, Harold," I said in mock exasperation, "and, if you must know, it's just like that Green Machine of yours that has a butt like a Christmas tree ornament."

With that I doubled up the pressure on the fish, "putting the wood to him," as they say. After I got him turned, he was not long coming in. I waded out into knee-deep water and tailed him.

"He's a beauty! He'll go seven pounds at least," Harold said. "No need to put the tape on him, he's legal." But I did anyway, measuring him out against the small cloth dressmaker's tape I carried.

"Twenty-four inches," I announced, elated that I somehow had beaten Harold at his own game.

"Nice fish. You going to fish through the run again, Mike?"

"Got that right! And with a bug!"

CHAPTER 2

The History of the Bug

I am not the first to develop the principles of bug fishing, nor am I the only one who has researched certain components of the method. The pattern itself developed over many decades, and much of the work on presentation had been laid down long before I was born by such distinguished writers and anglers as Wood and Skues (although they did not apply their ideas to the discipline of bug fishing). Fly fishing for trout and salmon originated in the British Isles, but there appears to have been little, if any, exchange of ideas or information between North American and British salmon anglers in this century. Apart from the revolutionary tactics of the greased line method of Arthur Wood, the radical departures from traditional salmon fishing took place on the rivers of Canada. The list includes dry fly fishing, the Patent method, the Portland hitch, the Hair-wings, and the development of the Bomber patterns which evolved into what are now simply known as bugs.

Deer Hair Flies

The hair of northern deer, moose and caribou, collectively known as "deer hair," has a unique quality. The material is hollow, and the air inside the shaft insulates the animal from the extreme cold of winter. Being hollow, deer hair also has superior flotation qualities, and for this reason it is the foundation for a variety of salmon patterns simply known as bugs.

The use of deer hair to create a fishing lure is not new. The Indians of North America used strips of deer hide, fur and all, as a bass lure. In her book *The Yearling*, set in Florida's Everglades, Marjorie Kinnan Rawlings describes how deer hair would be tied to a hook to create a "bob," which was dapped and skittered amongst the lily pads to catch bass. I read *The Yearling* long before my introduction to salmon fishing; I was ten years old at the time and lived at the foot of the Lachine Rapids in Montreal, Quebec, a good five hundred miles away from the nearest salmon river. All I knew about Atlantic salmon came from a picture and short description in *The Golden* Nature Guides: Fishes, a pocket-sized book familiar to kids growing up in the 1950s.

About 1901, Dr. James A. Henshall, of Cincinatti, Ohio, created clipped multicoloured deer hair bass bugs. The flotation qualities of the material helped to produce an outstanding surface lure for largemouth and smallmouth bass. Dr. Henshall's success certainly brought into

Muddler Minnow

The History of the Bug

focus the potential of deer hair for fly tyers. Many patterns have evolved since, such as the streamer patterns Thunder Creek and Muddler Minnow, and dry flies such as Rat Face McDougall and the Irresistibles (which were used for Atlantic salmon long before the introduction of the Bomber).

During the 1920s, F. Gray Griswold fished the Grand Cascapedia, Quebec. It is recorded that, using his deer hair bug creations, he landed two salmon of 25 and 32 pounds. How the bugs were fished is a matter of conjecture, and it must be remembered that using something as revolutionary as bass bugs on tradition-bound salmon waters was not the norm. With the passage of time, Griswold's patterns were forgotten until Father Smith's reintroduction of sorts on the Nashwaak.

Irresistible

A pattern in existence at about the same time as Griswold's bug was the Devil or Cooper's Bug, which is still tied commercially in New England. It somewhat resembles the bug used today in salmon fishing, but it has a chenille body overlapped with deer hair. Its configuration is not unlike the Bomber. Tied in the style of the Humpy dry fly but without the wings and hackle, the pattern was developed and used for the Adirondack brook trout caught in New York state. It is only natural to assume that the Devil or Cooper's Bug would be in the fly

Devil Bug

boxes of anglers travelling north to the salmon rivers of Atlantic Canada and Maine, and perhaps these migrant bugs planted the seed of an idea that would come to maturity some sixty years later.

Bug Patterns

Chance could have played a part in the development of the bug. It is easy to imagine a pattern such as the Irresistible being stripped of its wings and hackle as the result of a low back cast, accidentally becoming an effective bug pattern that would not ride high in the water. The angler, upon landing a salmon, might never suspect that an alteration he failed to notice was the reason for his success; he might attribute the mangled fly instead to his battle with the fish.

Among established fly patterns, the closest in appearance to the bug pattern are some western flies such as the Zulu and the Woolly Worm. Utilizing peacock herl and wool for the body, both are highly effective trout patterns; both are usually weighted. (Don't forget that using weighted flies invites prosecution on the charge of jigging; these flies are illegal in designated salmon waters.)

Woolly Worm

About the only established salmon pattern that resembles the modern-day bug is one from the British Isles that made its appearance in the 1800s. Called the Grub or the Usk Grub, it did not incorporate deer body hair as its foundation.

The History of the Bug

The first reference I can recall to a predecessor of a bug pattern was in a 1970 article in which it was named a Cigar Butt. Now known as a Bomber, it had a body of natural deer hair spun and clipped to shape, a short stub tail of deer hair, and a brown hackle palmered the length of the body. It was tied on a wide gap #6 streamer hook, and was claimed as a panacea for the low water conditions on the Miramichi.

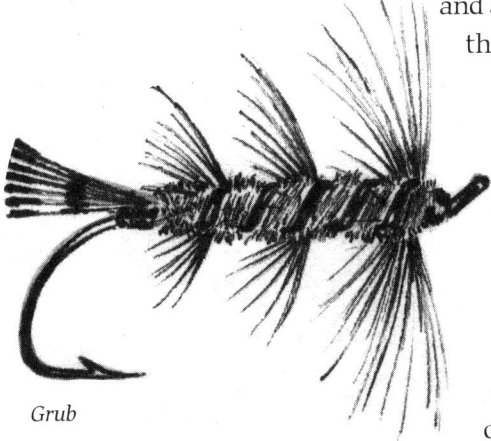

Here and there, bugs of a sort were being used outside the main salmon-angling circles. These were local phenomena, and I suspect that, being highly productive, they remained closely guarded secrets.

Grub

The Musquodoboit River winds its way through the low limestone hills of Nova Scotia's eastern shore about sixty miles from Halifax. A small river of short interconnecting runs and deep peat-stained still waters, it produces some salmon, particularly some fine spring-run fish, averaging about 14 pounds, yielding perhaps 20 to 30 fish in a good year. (Later in August there is a small grilse run.) I fished the river infrequently in the early seventies and did not really come to know it well, but I remember an angler from the little village of Meaghers Grant who fished the river regularly and enjoyed considerable success. He used a fly of his own creation that he called a Dobit, a name I took to be derived from the river's name.

I believe that the Dobit pattern was an independent development. It was tied on a #4 single, with a short tail of white calf tail and a spun white deer hair body, clipped to a stubby cylindrical shape and finished with a sparse hackle collar of grizzly and orange. As the holding water was narrow, the Meaghers Grant angler fished the fly almost directly downstream. Seldom were his casts more than twenty feet. Cast slightly to one side of the lie, the fly had a short drift before it submerged. It was at this point that it would induce a rise. I never quite mastered the technique and had no success with the patterns. In the coming years they lay forlorn in an all-but-forgotten fly box.

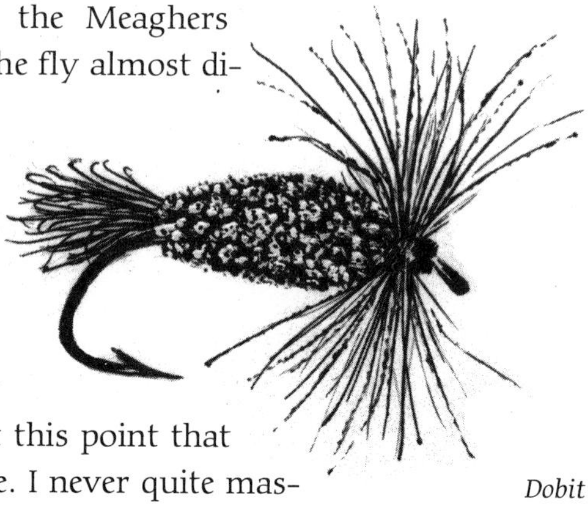

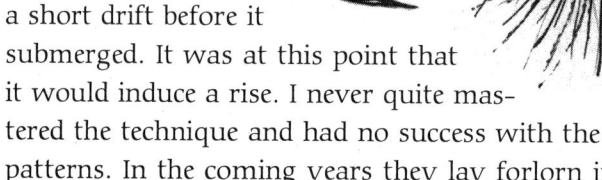

Dobit

In 1965, Father Elmer Smith, of Prince William, New Brunswick, introduced to the Miramichi and the Atlantic salmon an effective pattern that would have far-ranging consequences: the Bomber. The tactic was to fish the pattern dry on a bagged line that would swing the fly on an arc, creating a surface commotion as it skimmed across the surface. The creation of the Whiskers pattern, attributed to a local Miramichi fly tier, was a refinement of the basic Bomber that improved upon the skittering process.

Somewhat later, in 1970, Father Smith developed and used the first bug patterns, supposedly on New Brunswick's Nashwaak River. The Nashwaak is primarily a dry fly or bug river until late in September, when the fall rains swell the river's volume and large wet flies and streamers become outstanding pro-

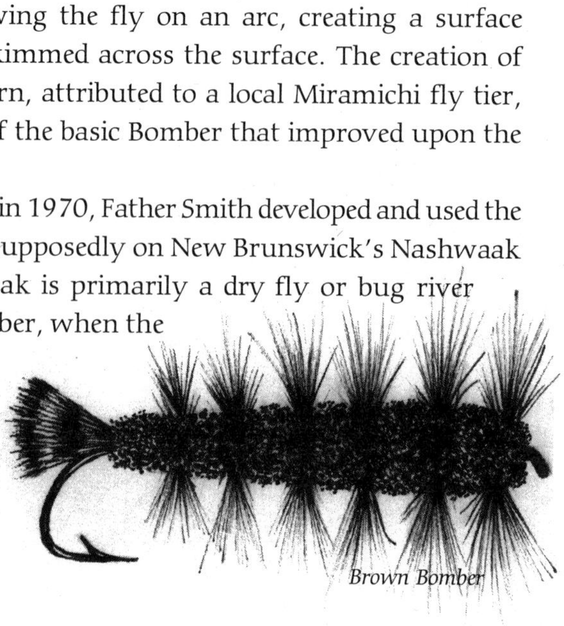

Brown Bomber

ducers. In the beginning, Father Smith's patterns were nothing more than scaled-down versions of the Bomber, which were fished as dry flies. Some of Father Smith's fellow anglers recall with awe the deadly effectiveness with which he used his bugs. Thus the Buck Bug, or the Bug as it is more commonly known, made its appearance on the angling scene. Only when I began to fish the rivers of southern New Brunswick in 1977 did I encounter the pattern of today's bug.

While the credit should go to Father Smith for his introduction of the Bomber and the Buck Bug, he was not the first to successfully employ a bug pattern for Atlantic salmon. What Father Smith did accomplish, however, was this: he brought into focus the qualities of deer hair as a superb material with which to tie a variety of salmon patterns, and he launched a method of presentation with which to fish them successfully.

Buck Bug

In the years that followed, the metamorphosis of the Bomber into the Buck Bug pattern, along with correspondingly refined tactics, charted a new course in salmon angling. At first, the Bomber was fished as a dry fly. Later it was downsized into the form of today's bug. In the beginning, the bug, too, was fished as a dry fly. By happenstance, some anglers found it was more effective fished wet on a standard wet fly cast. Then someone discovered that, when the bug was presented as a nymph, cast somewhat upstream and across the current on a dead drift, it became deadly effective in the hands of those practitioners who fished them thus.

Nymphs

In 1857, W.C. Stewart, a solicitor in Edinburgh, Scotland, published *The Practical Angler*. Although Stewart advocated the imitative nymphal pattern, an evolution from the standard wet fly of his day, he was also the first to advocate the fishing of wet flies upstream. Some fifty years later, George Edward MacKenzie Skues, the father of modern nymph tactics, revived Stewart's principles and adapted them to the dead drift of certain nymphal forms in order to take the selective brown trout of the British chalk streams.

Skues stressed realism of the patterns and their presentation; different nymphal forms behaved differently according to the species they imitated. He popularized his ideas in many articles and books, the main ones being *Minor Tactics of the Chalk Stream* (1910), *The Way of a Trout With a Fly* (1921), and *Nymph Fishing for Chalkstream Trout* (1939). Detailed in terms of entomology and tactics, these books rivalled the works of Frederick Halford, the father of dry fly fishing. Ernest Schwiebert coined the phrase that summarizes Skues's theory: the angler must "match the hatch." As well as his book *Matching the Hatch*, Schwiebert also authored the definitive work to date on nymphs and nymphing, *Nymphs* (1973).

Could deer hair be used to create nymphal patterns? In my estimation, this possibility has been entirely overlooked. Traditional nymphal patterns and their modern counterparts place a very strong emphasis on sinkability and realism. The bug resembles a stone fly nymph, the basic shape being somewhat cylindrical and tapered at both ends, but here the similarity ends. When thoroughly soaked, the bug does not sink but is predisposed towards a state of neutral buoyancy. Its attractors and size preclude its use in the purest circles of traditional trout nymphing. I would, however, hazard a guess that it would produce outstanding results if tied to nymph specifications of realism and fished as a subsurface presentation. Deer hair nymph bodies could combine varying shades of hair, sculpted to the selectivity of the trout species sought. When tied, deer hair flares and can be spun on the hook. It can be trimmed with fine-edged scissors to the shape of a bug, which has the same basic form as most nymphal patterns.

Nymphal patterns are not new to salmon circles. Charles DeFeo, a professional artist from New York City, was also an innovative fly tier who adapted established trout nymph patterns into a line of salmon nymphs. DeFeo used these successfully on the Miramichi in the 1950s. Tied to salmon specifications of hook size and type, they essentially imitate nymphal forms and are designed to sink. In his book *The Atlantic Salmon*, Lee Wulff admits to having tried these nymphs with some success, using them in combination with trout tactics.

DeFeo Salmon Nymph

Casting Methods

In Britain, between 1900 and 1930, Arthur H.E. Wood developed the method of fishing a reduced wet fly dressing as a subsurface presentation to salmon by using a greased line: a silk fly line oiled so it would float. His method was to cast the fly slightly upstream and to mend the drift frequently so that the fly pulsed up and down to the lie of the salmon. It must be remembered that while Wood was fishing traditional wet flies on a downstream arc, his introduction of the floating fly line laid the foundation not only for dry fly fishing, but also for bugging for salmon. Today, few salmon anglers fish with sinking tip lines and fewer still with sinking lines. The floating fly lines now used for dry flies, wet flies or bugs owe their use in salmon fishing to Wood.

Meanwhile, in the 1920s, on the Restigouche River, Colonel Lewis S. Thompson developed the Patent method of fishing for salmon. Essentially, a large wet fly was cast upstream and allowed to drift downstream on a slack line. With the current straightening out the cast, the line tightened and the sunken fly would rise, inducing a take. The method proved its worth. But, although it introduced a new technique to the realm of salmon angling, it was not bug fishing, as the use of a slack line might suggest.

Bugging the Atlantic Salmon

Nymphing for Atlantic salmon became bugging when the tactics of Wood, Skues and Thompson were combined with a fly that had the tendency *neither* to sink nor to float.

The principal of neutral buoyancy is the heart of bug fishing. You can illustrate this for yourself: you'll need a tall beaker of water and a bug and a wet fly of similar size. Soak both flies thoroughly. Place them both at the surface of the water in the beaker and watch what happens. Though this is not a precise scientific experiment, you will see the wet fly sink about four times as fast as the bug.

Without that neutral buoyancy, the bug would not be unique. Instead, one would be fishing a wet fly or a dry fly or a nymph. Bug fishing incorporates elements of all three. In slow to moderate currents, standard wet fly patterns have a tendency to hang down perpendicular, while a bug rides more horizontally, thus presenting the fish with a more balanced, active view of the fly. The depth at which the bug rides is determined by the incline of the angle of the leader to the floating fly line. The longer the leader, the closer to the surface the bug will drift; the shorter the leader, the deeper the bug will ride.

Bug fishing can be summed up as fishing a pattern having the quality of neutral buoyancy, in the style of Wood's greased line method, coupled with Skue's tactic of casting across and slightly upstream to achieve dead drift and a subsurface presentation. If the pattern begins to skim or ride the surface, the presentation has developed drag; the angler should mend the line to eliminate it and achieve a controlled drift, but mending should be done only as required. This procedure lets the bug ride the subsurface element of the current, undulating with every movement of the river's flow toward the salmon resting in the lie. I believe this slow, deliberate approach to the fish triggers the feeding response the fish developed as a parr.

When I lived in Nova Scotia, I fished the small rivers flowing into Minas Basin: the Stewiacke, Salmon, North, Debert, Folly, Great Village, Portapique, Economy, Five Island and Maccan rivers. The clarity and depth of the waters allowed me to view this feeding phenomenon closely. During the first runs, in the first week of September, I would use small wet flies, #8s and #10s. Casting above the lie, I would observe the fly swinging on its arc toward the fish. As the fly came into the salmon's view, the fish would become agitated. It would rock from side to side, gauging the speed and range needed to make the interception. At times, the white mouth lining would show as the gill covers began to work. At this stage, the fish would either swing out and forward and rise to the fly or swing briefly out of the lie, only to retreat again. More than once I watched the fish rise and then return to its station, allowing the fly to pass by. After a pause, the salmon would turn decisively right or left, depending where it saw the fly, and drop downstream. (The first time I saw this, I believed I had spooked the fish from its lie.) Just before the fly slowed on the completion of its swing, the fish would curve in from behind and take.

This feeding phenomenon throws light on a common fly-fishing problem. An angler raises a fish and immediately casts again to the exact position where the rise occurred. More often than not, he cannot induce the fish to rise again. What the angler does not realize is that the salmon has left its original position and returned to it. Casting to where the rise was noted places the fly beyond where the fish can see it. As a general rule, note where your initial cast is placed. If you do raise a fish, duplicate the cast and the current will deliver the fly over the fish.

The same phenomenon may explain the "double take." I am sure that many anglers can recall having seen a salmon rise or boil to the fly, the surface calm only to be disturbed again by a take some distance from the first rise. Often a salmon will take a well-presented bug in the classic head and tail rise. What the angler usually notices is the back of the salmon out of the water. Rises are not usually splashy (because of the minimal surface disturbance, many times what I thought was a grilse has turned out to be a salmon). This is not to say that salmon do not smack bugs with an extreme prejudice, for they do so in the swifter runs when bugs are fished as wet flies. As water levels drop and warm, bug fishing comes into its own, the fish being leisurely in their upstream migration as well as in their takes.

Watching successful bug fishermen was a learning experience for me. They do not present the bug pattern in the same manner as they would wet flies. Bug presentation appears to be an unconscious effort, with a cast placed across and slightly upstream, quite unlike the standard 45-degree-angle downstream wet fly cast. Actually, up and across is a time-honoured method of fishing nymphs. Most salmon anglers, when asked why they fish a bug differently, will invariably answer, "Because that is how I fish this particular lie." It is part of the approach to a certain stretch of water with a particular bug.

The History of the Bug

Hartland Salmon Pool, on the upper St. John River, about 1938. Note that one angler has a split cane rod and the other has a 14' solid ash rod. Beechwood Dam, built in the 1960s, lies some twenty miles upstream from the Hartland Salmon Pool. PROVINCIAL ARCHIVES OF NEW BRUNSWICK P93CA4B

The approach has produced fish in the past, and the anglers are confident that it will do so again. If you ask them whether they have tried to alter or interchange their tactics, the response will invariably be that they have, and that it usually doesn't work.

We are creatures of habit and are loath to change. In most cases, anglers successfully employing a body of knowledge collectively known as bug fishing have never so much as opened a book on the tactics of nymphing. They simply carry on with a method that works, for, as the adage says, "If it ain't broke, don't fix it."

No. 6XL Bombers. Note the small body diameters. These are designed to be fished like bugs. DANIEL BATE-BOEROP

CHAPTER 3

The Pattern

A majority of salmon anglers do not tie their own flies, believing that even the modern reduced dressings are beyond their capabilities. I would tend to agree, since mastering the art of fly tying even to a limited extent takes a good deal of time, patience, and above all practice. Be that as it may, a beginner can create effective bug patterns after a few tries. Home-tied bugs, even when they lack commercial fineness of trim and look quite bedraggled, nevertheless account for their share of salmon.

Bug patterns (including Bombers, which are sparse of hackle and have small body diameters) are among the easiest salmon patterns to tie. They are durable and effective, and their productivity tends to increase in direct proportion to the degree of rattiness they achieve after prolonged use. Do not be too hasty in discarding a bug that has had its hackle stripped off, not an uncommon occurrence. I have often returned a favourite bug to the fly-tying vice. After cutting through the head and unwinding the thread from the body, you can easily tie in a new hackle. I am loath to throw away a fly unless the hook is broken.

I would like to mention hook quality here. I favour bronzed tempered steel hooks, manufactured by Mustad and by Partridge, of Redditch, England. The traditional black iron hooks used in tying wet flies are heavier, requiring a greater diameter of spun deer hair to keep them from sinking too deeply. This requirement of course alters the size and proportions of the fly. If you don't tie your own flies, do spend the extra money for fly patterns tied on good quality hooks. The stickiness of a hook point is usually indicative of quality. Gently touch the point with your fingertip; if it sticks to your finger, it's sharp, and the sharpness shows it's made from tempered steel.

Green Machine

This method of tying the bug pattern helps to ensure that the overall size is not too large. It allows for the full exposure of the spear, which, unhindered by body materials, can make for a more secure hook set. In texture, deer hair is somewhat akin to the soft side of Velcro, acting much the same way when it comes into contact with the salmon's teeth. Thus the hair aids in preventing the salmon from ejecting the bug easily.

Materials:

    Hook: #6 Partridge D4A #2X Streamer Hook, DTE Bronze
    Deer hair: Green
    Hackle: Coachman Brown, medium stiffness.
    Butt: Fluorescent green and red wool or floss
    Thread: 6/0 green monocord

STEP 1: Clamp the hook in the vice and attach the thread to the shank in line with the point of the hook. Wind back along the shank until the thread is in line with the barb. Separate the strands from a 4" section of green

The Pattern

fluorescent wool. Tie one piece on top of the shank. (This strand will serve to lock the butt into place and help prevent unravelling.) Advance the thread $\frac{1}{8}$". Tie in another strand of green fluorescent wool. (*Fig. 1*)

STEP 2: Carefully wind the wool backwards along the shank, then forwards, then backwards again, and so on, to build up the butt. (Too much tension will cause the wool to separate. This is one reason that some fly tiers prefer fluorescent floss.) Secure with a half hitch. Grasping the wool strand at the base of the shank, bring it forward over the butt. Secure with a half hitch. The green butt section is now complete. Using red fluorescent wool, repeat Step 2 and secure with a couple of half hitches. Each fully formed butt should be approximately $\frac{1}{8}$" in length and of even proportions. (*Fig. 2*)

STEP 3: Select a small tuft of green deer hair, and with forefinger and thumb strip out the fuzz. Lay the clump of deer hair along the shank at the point where the red fluorescent butt has been secured. Position the hair so that the thread will bisect the clump. Still holding the hair with thumb and forefinger, loop the thread over twice. (*Fig. 3*)

STEP 4: With slow, steady tension, tighten down the thread. The clump of hair will begin to revolve and flare up. Continue wrapping forward through the clump. When there is no more hair to flare, secure with a half hitch. (*Fig. 4*)

STEP 5: Repeat the process until a collar of hair is formed along the shank to a point $\frac{1}{8}$" from the eye. Tie off with a couple of half hitches, cut the thread and remove bug from vice. (*Fig. 5*)

Bugging the Atlantic Salmon

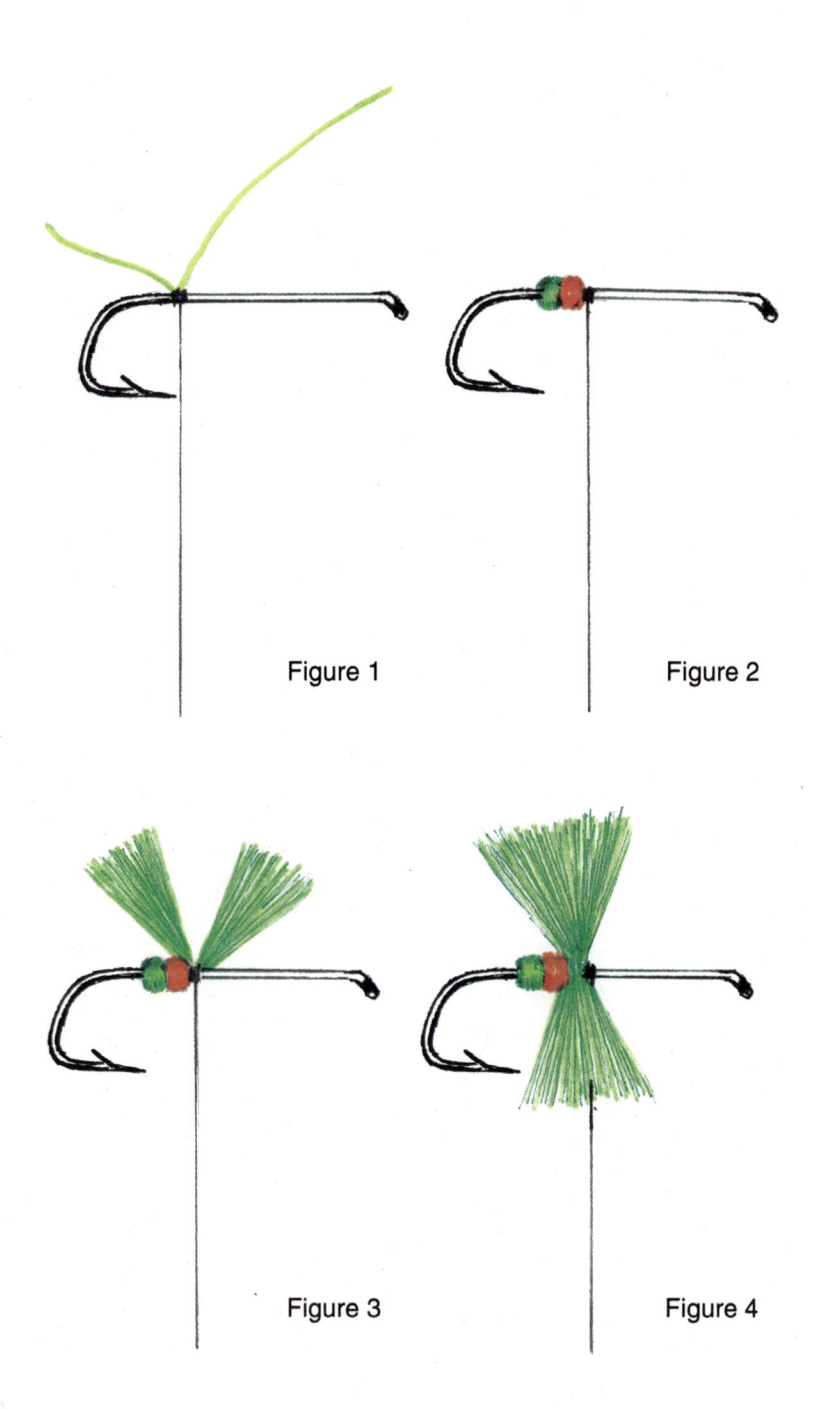

Figure 1

Figure 2

Figure 3

Figure 4

The Pattern

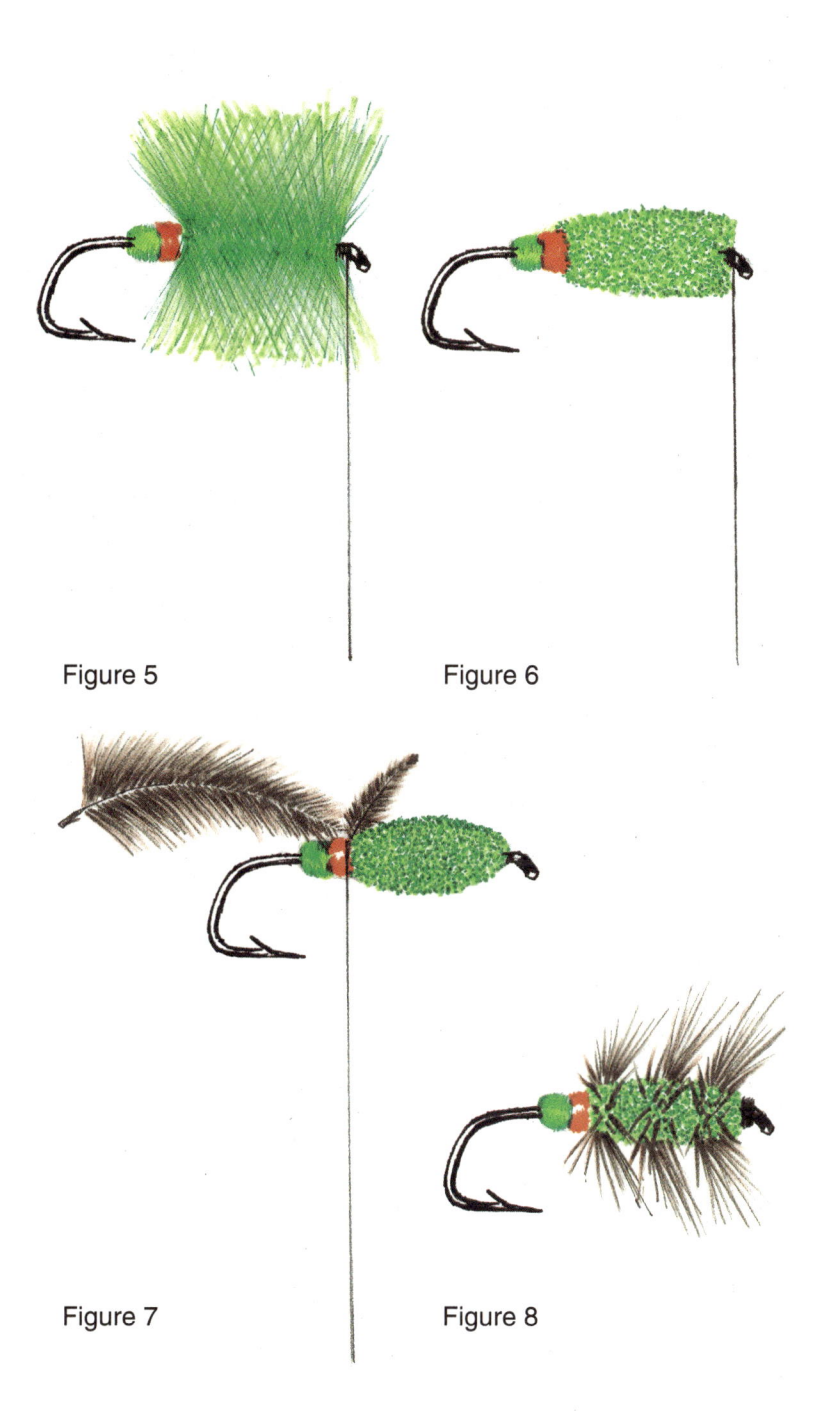

Figure 5

Figure 6

Figure 7

Figure 8

STEP 6: Using a pair of fine curved cuticle scissors, trim away at the collar beginning at the butt, cutting up and down to expose it. It will now be much easier to gauge proportions and form a body slightly tapered at both ends. Trim the collar until the thickest part of the body is three to four times the diameter of the butt. With a little practice, you can easily achieve these proportions. Remember, bugs are constructed to have neutral buoyancy, so too little trimming will make it behave more like a dry fly. Return the bug to the vice. Reattach the thread to the shank below the hook eye with a couple of half hitches. Wind the thread through the body towards the butt, snugging down the threadas you go (there is no need for finely spaced wrapping). (*Fig. 6*)

STEP 7: Select a brown Coachman hackle of medium dry fly quality. Avoid webby hen hackle because it will give the bug a bulky appearance. The length of the hackle should not exceed the gap of the hook. Place the tip of the hackle at the base of the deer hair body and wrap down, meshing the tip into the body hair. Apply a small drop of thin head cement. Advance the tying thread to the eye. With hackle pliers, grip the butt of the feather, winding the hackle forward through the body, Palmer style, to the eye. Alternatively, you can tie in the butt section of the hackle first. (*Fig. 7*)

STEP 8: Tie down. Trim excess hackle and whip finish. Apply two coats of clear head cement. (*Fig. 8*)

The Pattern

Favoured Bug Patterns

Hooks: #6, #8 and #10, bronzed 2X
Styles: Sproat or Model Perfect
Threads: Coloured monocord 6/0

Green Machine Variant:
Same as Green Machine, except the red and green butt is replaced with a tuft of white rabbit fur.

Plain Brown:
Tag: Three wraps of medium gold oval tinsel
Tail: Two golden pheasant tippets, tied so as not to exceed the hook's bend in length
Butt: None
Body: Brown deer hair
Hackle: Coachman brown

Electric Banana:
Butt: Orange fluorescent wool
Body: Yellow deer hair
Hackle: Orange
Electric Bananas are usually tied on XL streamer hooks up to 4" long

Black Bug:
Butt: Small bright orange wool butt
Body: Black deer hair
Hackle: Orange

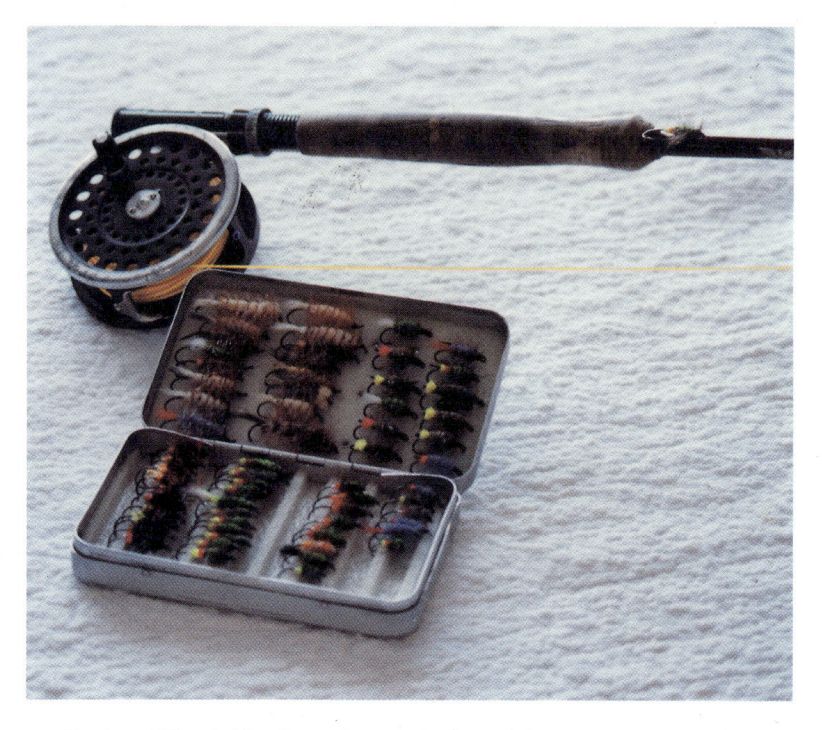

Bugging the Atlantic Salmon

A collection of flies tied by the author. At the upper left are No. 6XL Bombers. The rest are all Bugs. DANIEL BATE-BOEROP

Glitter Bug:
Tail: Krystal Hair (Flashabou), various colours, 5 or 6 strands
Body: Natural deer hair
Hackle: Brown

Snowball:
Butt: Fluorescent orange wool
Body: White deer hair
Hackle: Orange

The Pattern

Deer hair body used to create the emergence stage of a caddis fly nymph.
DANIEL BATE-BOEROP

Smurf:
Butt: Red fluorescent wool
Body: Blue deer hair
Hackle: Blue or brown

Standards:
Butt: Red or green fluorescent wool
Body: Natural or brown deer hair
Hackle: Coachman brown
Tail: Optional, replacing the butt: 3 or 4 strands of either red or green fluorescent wool, ⅛" to ¼" in length

Bugging the Atlantic Salmon

In tying bugs, the colour spectrum is limited only by one's imagination. I have found the suggested colour combinations successful, but in some river systems different colours may be more productive than others, the fish showing a decided preference for one over another. I myself favour the green and natural deer hair bodies.

It is common knowledge that salmon can be very selective. Even though rivers are but a few miles apart, preference for a specific fly pattern may be marked by such subtle differences as size and configuration. Though this is dependent to a great degree on water clarity and temperature, it is well known that the salmon of North America show a willingness to rise to a dry fly on some rivers, while it is said that their European counterparts will not. The records of fish taken on a dry fly from Ireland, the United Kingdom and Iceland waters are considered rarities. As to the rivers of northern Europe, almost nothing has been documented that I am aware of. Naturally, this makes me wonder just how effective bugs might be on the rivers of Europe. I hope that one day I may be fortunate enough to fish these rivers with bugs, trusting that I won't upset local conventions by doing so. In the meantime, should anglers have the opportunity to fish for European salmon with bugs, I would be most interested to learn of their success or failure. Correspondence should be addressed to: Michael W. Brislain, c/o Goose Lane Editions, 469 King Street, Fredericton NB Canada E3B 1E5.

CHAPTER 4

Gone Bugging

Before you think about fishing for Atlantic salmon in New Brunswick, you need to know that the salmon rivers of the province are designated as Crown Reserve, Crown Open and Leased. These terms denote access, and they may also have specific sections designated for hook and release only.

Only Crown Open water has unrestricted access for both resident and non-resident anglers; non-residents are required by law to have a registered guide while angling for salmon. It should be noted that most salmon rivers are scheduled, meaning that only fly fishing is allowed on those waters at specified times. Thus the only legal way to angle for Atlantic salmon is by fly fishing.

In New Brunswick, the current season limit is eight grilse, less than 25" (63 cm) in length. The daily limit is two fish. All fish must be tagged. Any salmon over 25" must be returned to the river unharmed. Hook and release regulations may vary from river to river and from year to year. New Brunswick salmon angling regulations are comprehensive and detailed, and anglers are responsible for fully informing themselves. Contact the Department of Natural Resources and Energy, Government of New Brunswick, PO Box 6000, Fredericton NB Canada E3B 5H1.

Bombed!

I cannot confirm the truth of this story, but, knowing salmon fishermen as I do, I find it entirely plausible.

Nineteen-eighty was the first year in which the government of New Brunswick introduced a system of tagging fish as a way of preventing the movement and sale of poached salmon. Many anglers had problems complying with the law because the tags were adhesive-backed. They were to be wrapped around the tail of all salmon that were to be retained, but when they got wet they would not stay in place. So new guidelines were issued requiring anglers to make a small incision in the wrist section above the tail, insert the tag through the slit, and tie a knot.

Every time Gordon was scheduled to arrive at a certain fishing camp, Bob, the camp manager, would get that sinking feeling in the pit of his stomach. He would take Lyman, his head guide, aside. This was an annual ritual for both, Bob admonishing Lyman that he had a responsibility to the camp and his sport, and that, as head guide, he should set an example of decorum and excellence for the other guides.

Lyman would of course listen intently, nodding his head in agreement at the appropriate times. "Yes, Bob, you're *absolutely* right." "That were pretty shameful, what happened last year." "Was right to fire me." "'Twere no excuse."

In 1980, his sermon over, Bob walked away to the main lodge, talking to himself and wondering what effect it would have on Lyman this time. Well, at least he had discharged his responsibility. Their troubles were just as much Gordon's fault as Lyman's. What a pair those two were — like kids.

Gordon was nothing short of a millionaire many times over, yet he was as down to earth as any man could be. In his late fifties, he was small in stature, balding, but with a heart as big as the river itself. With a share of this lease on the Restigouche,

Gone Bugging

his hunting lodge in Colorado, and his tarpon water in Costa Rica, he alternated his free time as the seasons dictated and as his wife would tolerate. His flint-grey eyes struck terror on Wall Street and yet twinkled with mischievous merriment once they were far away from the corporate office.

Lyman was the exact opposite, a big man 20 years Gordon's junior. His slow speech belied his native cunning. His most obvious features were a great shock of unruly red hair and huge callused hands. His thumbs alone were as thick as hoe handles, inset with thick chisel-like nails. Hard work in the woods each winter since he was a boy of 14 had moulded these hands, yet they could exquisitely craft a #10 Rusty Rat or cast a fly line as if it were a gossamer thread. Lyman was considered to be the best guide on the Restigouche. It was said he could get salmon for his sports when nobody else could. He knew the river in all its moods, and he shared the river's secrets, including the hidey-holes in the rapids where salmon would lie.

The love of two things brought this unlikely pair together: the sport of salmon fishing and Scotch whisky.

Gordon's arrival was like Santa Claus coming on the Fourth of July, all wrapped up in a big red ribbon. He headed directly for the guide shack. "Hello, Bob, how have you been, glad to see you. Yes, good flight from New York, bit of a problem in Fredericton with my baggage. For a while I though I had lost my rod case. How's your good wife? I'm sure looking forward to some of that great cooking of hers."

"She's fine, Gordon, and we're glad to have you with us again this year," Bob answered.

"Here," said Gordon, handing Bob an envelope stuffed with American fifties. "I'd like you to look after everyone after I leave. And this is for you and the missus."

"Gordon, this isn't necessary, and we won't accept it, and that's final. Your Christmas gift was more than enough, I don't know how we can ever thank you for all your help. If Joan hadn't got into the Leahy Clinic in Boston, she'd still be having those terrible headaches."

"Well, I was happy to do it. What the hell's a man worth if he can't help people he cares about. And by the way, that box of salmon flies you sent for Christmas was just about the nicest thing you could have done. Some of those traditional feather wings you and your son Mike tied I've had mounted in a glass display case, and it's hanging on my boardroom wall."

"So, where's Lyman, Bob? Has he been behaving himself?"

"Now, Gordon, I've talked to Lyman and I hope you two don't get yourself into something you can't get out of. He's down by the landing, he should be up in a few moments."

Gordon made the rounds, being sure to greet and say hello to everyone, and by the time he left the main lodge and the kitchen the camp was in an uproar.

"Lyman! How in the hell have you been?"

"Never better, Gordon. I'm glad to see you. There's some big fish holding in Pine Ledge Rapids, and I think we should have some pretty fair sport, fishing those big Bombers wet."

Gordon slapped his knees in delight at the news. "All right, that's just what I wanted to hear." Arms over each others' shoulders, the conspirators laughed their way to the kitchen.

Bob sighed. "I wonder what mischief those two will get into this time."

"Care for a drink, Lyman?" Gordon pulled the case of Chivas Regal from the trunk of his rental car. "No thanks, Gordon. At least not here in the camp. Bob says I gotta watch myself. You know what happened last year."

"Well, it wasn't your fault, Lyman, no matter what Bob said."

"I was s'pose to be guiding, Gordon, and running those rapids pissed to the gills could've got us both drownded."

"Well, it didn't. Besides, it was my idea to run the course at full throttle. Damn! That was quite a ride. Too bad we lost the fish," said Gordon.

"Damned if it wasn't! Fish or no fish, you didn't hear Bob on the other end on the line when I told him to send down the pickup truck 'cause we took the bottom clean out of the canoe. Course you were so happy nawth'n much made any impression on you."

Gordon started to chuckle when he remembered the look on Lyman's face at the instant when the jagged tooth of ledge ripped and splintered canvas and cedar. To Gordon, life was one big adventure; he was one of those rare individuals whom nothing fazes.

"Here, now, come on and have a drink. We have a lot of catching up to do before morning, and I *particularly* want to hear about those Bombers fished wet."

"Maybe just a touch." Lyman passed over his enamelled coffee mug and the light amber nectar of the gods splashed gently to the rim. Two fingers of Scotch to Gordon meant two fingers standing straight up, not lying horizontal.

So begins the story that has since become legend. The next morning found both Gordon and Lyman a little hazy. A good breakfast and many mugs of strong tea cleared the cobwebs, and the trip downriver was uneventful. The Pine Ledge Pool lies between upper and lower shelves of ledge rock that are called rapids but are in fact swift-flowing glides whose waters surge amid the boulders and outcroppings of the bottom strata. The pool itself is but a small area, approximately thirty feet by seventy feet, in which salmon would lie as they rested between the two runs. Hooking a big fish here meant a battle waged over a precipitous journey downstream.

After Gordon and Lyman had fished a good part of the morning, they landed one grilse. It was cause enough to celebrate.

From under the bow Gordon pulled open his canvas grab-bag and produced a bottle to toast the first fish. Within half an hour both men were glowing.

Gordon had been fishing a big white Bomber and suggested that he change flies, but Lyman insisted that he keep using it.

"Gordon, I think there's a big salmon lying up against that boulder about fifteen feet down from us. Give it a while, and if nawth'n happens we'll change flies."

Gordon knew better than to argue with Lyman, for he was seldom wrong about such things. But 10 minutes passed, and Gordon and Lyman agreed that it was time to change flies. Quickly reeling in toward were he sat in the bow, Gordon lifted the fly from the water just as a salmon charged it. The power of the rise carried the hooked fish clear of the water. It thudded right into the canoe, which rocked and threatened to upset.

Now, technically, this was a legal fish. Stunned and quivering at Gordon's feet, it was the biggest salmon he had ever hooked—it must have been in the 30-pound class. In that instant of simultaneous sobriety, a single thought ran through the men's minds: "Get a goddamn tag on it."

In that same moment, the salmon came alive and scooted toward the stern, its broad tail beating a steady tattoo. As they tried to wrestle the fish down in the narrow canoe, fly boxes, rods and seat cushions flew about and overboard.

"Stop fooling around with the fish, Gordon! That's it, grab him by the tail."

"That's what I'm trying to do! Jesus, do something Lyman, get the priest."

Finally the fish was pinned and was about to be dispatched.

Gordon and Lyman looked up a each other, an unspoken word passing between them. Without hesitation, they gently raised the struggling salmon and slipped it over the side.

"That was a trophy."

"Yes, and all of that. And nobody is going to believe this one."

Gone Bugging

"You're probably right, Lyman."

Disheartened only for a moment, Gordon peeled a paper tag away from the sheet, tossed it after the fish, and started to laugh.

"What the hell, Lyman, let's have a drink and toast the one that got away."

EQUIPMENT

Most of the revolutionary development in fishing tackle has taken place in North America. Gone are the days of finely crafted Tonkin split bamboo cane rods, King Eider silk fly lines and Spanish gut leaders. Rods of fibreglass, graphite and boron have now cornered the market. Fly lines of virtually indestructible vinyl composites have now replaced silk, which was prone to rot. These new lines will sink, float, or do both in varying degrees, depending on their specific density. New materials can be extruded to produce pre-tapered leaders with precision diameters.

Rods

The angler's choice of fly rods is virtually unlimited. They come in varying lengths, materials, and price ranges, designed to catch almost every species of game fish the active fly fisherman seeks. They range from the classic Tonkin split cane rod, built to exacting standards by the Orvis Company of Manchester, Vermont, to the Fenwick HMG Graphite, certainly one of the

Bugging the Atlantic Salmon

St. John River — 1900. Sunday afternoon at Hartt Pool, just below the Burpee Bar, Fredericton, New Brunswick. PROVINCIAL ARCHIVES OF NEW BRUNSWICK P5-348

most popular rods in use. At a cost of about $180 (as opposed to over $1000 for the Tonkin), the graphite rod has virtually replaced the split cane bamboo salmon rod for active use.

For perhaps a hundred years, split cane was the material of choice for fly rods, but before that, ash, greenheart, lancewood and hickory were used to construct solid salmon rods that could be 18 feet or more in length. The use of bamboo as a rod material is generally attributed to American violin and gun maker Samuel Phillippe, who first glued three triangular pieces of Calcutta split cane together to form a rod section. In 1880, Tonkin bamboo was discovered to have greater strength and elasticity. Hiram Lewis Leonard constructed six-sided rod blanks that by 1900 established the superiority of Tonkin bamboo, and it remained the favourite material for fly rods until the 1950s.

The split cane fly rod is now a collector's item. After World War II, a process was developed in which glass fibres were bonded with resins to produce fibreglass. Dr. Arthur Howland patented a fibreglass rod and demonstrated it to the Shakespeare Company, which secured the rights and began commercial production. Garcia Conolon introduced the first tubular glass rods a short while later. Between 1950 and 1970, various manufacturers effected a great many improvements in the quality of fibreglass rods, including a reduction in price.

The fibreglass rod became the norm, but this old standby has now largely been replaced by lighter, more powerful rods. In the 1970s, graphite began to make its presence felt on the angling scene, and today graphite rods are pretty much the standard amongst the salmon angling fraternity. Graphites can cast a line that reaches greater distances with less effort because the material delivers higher line speeds than fibreglass rods. Each year sees the development and marketing of new technology, such as the most recently introduced rod material, boron.

Regardless of cost and material, all fly rods are designed to accomplish the same things:

— to utilize the weight of the fly line to deliver an almost weightless object over a distance to a predetermined place;

— to act as a shock absorber, reducing the impact of the set and equalizing the stress to prevent the leader from snapping;

— to act as a lever against which the salmon strains, eventually exhausting its reserves of strength.

A good quality fly rod equipped with a good salmon reel can successfully bring to hand a 20-pound fish with a leader of 6-pound test.

I have a number of fly rods, including graphites, but when the waters warm and the current slows, I take down the old, battered rod case that contains my favourite rod for bugging a salmon — a Fenwick fibreglass FF 9010 5 oz., for a #10-weight line.

Purchased in 1981, the rod is now as battered as the case. The cracked ferrule has been reinforced with thread and epoxy. The grip is extensively pitted, and each winter I fill it with cork dust and lacquer. Some of the eyes are flattened, and the finish has been marred and chipped in numerous falls and other mishaps. But for all its unsightliness, I have yet to find a rod that is its equal for bugging the Atlantic salmon.

This rod would be technically classed as having a medium action, but I would say that it tends to be on the soft side. I found that it was not capable of lifting a 10-weight line to my satisfaction; many a backcast resulted in the line's collapsing on the forward cast. I had used a friend's rod of the same model and could find no fault with it, though he used a fly line of a different manufacture, one in which the body was probably somewhat shorter. I thought of writing to Fenwick to ask whether my rod had a design fault, but I never did so.

During July of the 1986 season, my favourite graphite rod was out of commission (I had not been quick enough to get the tip section out of the way of a closing door). Rather than begin an interchange of lines and reels, I mounted my Hardy Marquis 1 reel, loaded with WF9F and 150 yards of backing, to the Fenwick. I soon began to discover some amazing things.

The old fibreglass rod that could not handle a #10 did an outstanding job with a #9, with minimum effort and at a lower line speed than that generated by my invalided graphite. This rod was the perfect instrument with which to fish bugs.

Gone Bugging

Lower line speeds gave me a control and manoeuvrability that would be difficult to match in another type of rod. My goal became presentation, not distance.

For the same reason, a rod with slow action that flexes into the butt section is preferred by the experienced nymph fisherman in his quest for trout. While slowness in the flex eases and increases the accuracy of presentation, it does not significantly air-dry the moisture from the pattern. By comparison, a fly rod designed for dry fly fishing has an extremely fast taper that aids in the drying of the fly. With time and resources, I would certainly not hesitate to experiment with different rod blanks and materials, including graphite, to see if a salmon fly rod could be designed specifically for salmon bugging.

However, since no specific bugging rod exists, I recommend beginning with a glass rod 8 ½', 9' or 9 ½' long, one that flexes into the butt section and is classed as a medium action rod. You can establish this by shaking the rod from side to side, noting the point at which the flex in the rod begins. Ideally, it should begin in the upper portion of the butt section. Because today's marketing touts the principle of lighter rods handling greater line weights, there has been a tendency to "borderline" AFTMA (American Fishing Tackle Manufacturers Association) specifications in order to reduce rod weight classifications. I recommend going to one line size smaller than the manufacture's specification. You may find that your rod is more comfortable for casting while at the same time delivering your fly more accurately and over a greater distance.

Their are many excellent manufacturers of glass rods, among them Fenwick, Browning (which produced the Silaflex series), Abu Garcia, Diawa, Hardy, and Orvis. I will leave it to the individual to make his own selection. However, a rod specifically designed for nymphing, be it constructed from glass, graphite, boron or bamboo, would be a good start, provided it has the capacity to take on the Atlantic salmon.

Reels

A good salmon reel is essential, one that will hold 100 yards of 20-pound test Micron backing in addition to the fly line. In this type of angling, a large-capacity reel is not required unless the river being fished dictates otherwise. The lower portions of the St. John and the Restigouche in New Brunswick, the Humber in Newfoundland, and the Moise in Quebec provide expansive areas in which a hooked fish can run. A smooth drag system that will not freeze up or overspin is crucial. I have seen many a salmon lost when a reel seized, the leader parting with a snap.

Salmon reels vary in quality as they do in price. I have always preferred Hardy's St. John and Marquis 1. Pflueger makes a good durable fly reel, as does Rimfly. Of course, you can go to the other end of the spectrum to Bogdans, or you can even machine your own fly reels as does one angler that I know of in the Fredericton area. In any case, be particular in your choice of fly reels. Some inexpensive models may look especially well manufactured, but by the second season they may be out of commission, with the angler trying to locate a parts supplier.

Fly Lines

The fly lines most commonly used are those manufactured by Scientific Anglers and Cortland. The Scientific Anglers lines, especially their Air Cell Supreme, are a little stiffer in construction and feel than those of other manufacturers, but I find this quality suits my preference. Orvis has a very diversified product line, as do L.L. Bean and some of the other major tackle manufacturers and distributors.

I favour a weight forward over a double taper, mainly because anything over a #8 line size is usually difficult to acquire locally and can be obtained only by placing a special order. An 8 ½' Browning Silaflex rod with a DT8F served me well for many years. It was a pleasure to use this combination on the small intimate salmon streams of Nova Scotia's Colchester County, but it became limited for use on some of New Brunswick's larger rivers and fish.

Leaders

The leaders I use are in the 6-, 8- or 10-pound test category, constructed of Maxima leader materials. Usually, I use an 8-pound test throughout the season. Some anglers prefer a level leader of higher capacity, others construct their own tapered leaders, and still others purchase leaders pretapered. My own preference is for a leader that is about three feet longer than the rod length, approximately twelve feet overall, with a partial taper.

Using a nail knot, secure a 3-foot butt section of 20-pound test leader to the fly line. Coat the knot and about ¼" of the fly line with Pliobond. This helps to reinforce a potential weak spot against cracking, which could eventually lead to a break under strain. Use a blood knot to secure a 3-foot section of 15-pound test to the butt section; then to this section secure a 6-foot section of 6- or 8-pound test. You now have a leader that is somewhat tapered for ease of presentation, one that can be easily adapted as conditions (such as changing the tippet to one that is lighter or heavier) may warrant.

PRESENTATION & TACTICS

From the second week of July, 1988, through September of that year, low, warm water prevailed on many New Brunswick rivers. Only the occasional brief rains prevented critical conditions for the fish. The natural scheme of things was definitely upset. Old reliable patterns, even in smaller sizes and with reduced dressings, simply would not produce. From either imagination or desperation, fly tiers began bug production in a spectrum of colours and sizes to match the season: weird.

With patience and revaluation, and despite their lack of aesthetic appeal, the bugs began to yield fish when nothing else would. Even so, many anglers became frustrated with bugs that season, and their overeagerness made the frustration worse. There are those who still refuse to use the patterns because of the poor showing they had then. But the problem did not lie with the patterns but with the belief that bugs should be fished in the same manner as all wet flies.

Every angler has reminisced about seasons past, and in this introspection he generally finds some humour as well as valuable insights, even among the memories of years he once considered unmitigated disasters. In 1988, just before Christmas, I received a phone call from an old friend who wanted to wish me the season's best. Amid all the good-natured banter, the conversation quickly turned to Opening Day. We lamented the poor '88 season and fervently hoped '89 would not be a repeat.

After hanging up I sat back in one of those all-too-comfortable office chairs, the kind that make you feel more important than you really are. I was carried back to an incident that had occurred in August. It was a late Friday afternoon. The temperature was in the low nineties, with a humidity reading to match. The constant drone of the air conditioner was not exactly conducive to the preparation of financial statements. I debated whether to take in the evening's fish, but the alternative prospect, mowing the lawn, made up my mind. I put in a short phone call to a friend, and our plans were set.

As we drove upriver, muted grey thunderheads were building through the white haze that clung like a translucent curtain to the walls of the valley. The air was still. Far from ideal conditions for fishing, yet we hoped the promised rain would relieve the drought and ease the burden on the fish.

Emerging from the undergrowth, we came upon a grizzled old angler perched on a crooked finger of ledge that jutted into the main current of the pool. As we approached, I stopped in amazement when 40 feet of fly line sailed lazily over the riverside alders. Exasperated, the man turned in my direction, muttering something like, "Son of a whore, that's the fourth time he's risen, he's come half out taking short." Again he cast out and positioned himself like a sprinter in the starting blocks: bent forward, clutching the rod in a death grip, tense, eyes riveted to that one particular expanse of river where the bug would drift over the lie. As if on cue, the salmon broached broadside, lunging at the passing bug, and again the angler pulled up short. The quiet of the late afternoon was shattered by a blazing stream of invective peculiar to New Brunswickers, directed toward the fish and all creation. The man had lost control entirely. He stomped up the ledge to the bank, his determined effort to regain his composure including some enthusiastic turf kicking and rock scuffing.

As I neared him, I hesitantly began a somewhat one-sided conversation. "That's a big fish. What did you raise him on?"

"Smurf," came the curt reply.

The angler growled out something else, which I did not quite comprehend, and returned down the ledge to hammer out another cast. With a splat, the bug landed off the mark, some distance above the lie. A bit apologetic for his tone, but still attempting to focus on the drift, he turned aside to say in a voice that mirrored his despair, "I'm not having a good season 'tall. Only thing the fish'll look at are those #*$%*!# *BUGS*!!" *WHUMPH!* The sound was unmistakable, the slurp of a salmon inhaling a subsurface fly.

Feeling the bite, the fish turned into the heavy current. Racing downstream, it ran out of depth, exploding in a shower of foam and gravel. All our friend could do was hold the rod high as the fish swapped directions, the fly line slicing the current as it did so. After a short surface flurry and some wallowing, the salmon was grudgingly led into the shallows. Wading out to just above his knees, the angler with a deft left hand tailed a fish of about 20 pounds. With a practised twist he worked the fly out and released the fish unharmed.

Walking up to where we sat, grinning ear to ear, the angler was nattering away before he even reached us.

"Well, I'd never have believed it! Those bugs do work, and a blue one at that!" He admitted frankly that before catching this fish he had had little faith in bug patterns at all, having tried them to no effect over the years. With that, he packed up for home, leaving us to contemplate what we had witnessed, unaware that a valuable lesson had gone unnoticed.

Later, in the cooling twilight, fireflies began to wink in the tall grasses. Long shadows crept over the valley. Nighthawks buzz-bombed through the swarms of caddis flies lifting from the river, their nasal "peent" an enjoyable accompaniment to our quiet conversation. As we sat there going over the evening's fish, we realized that there was only one logical explanation for the old angler's success: "He got distracted just long enough for the fish to take."

The saying "Timing is everything" seemed appropriate to the occasion. Over the decades much has been written on the subject, and strong opinions on timing have been at the root of many a heated discussion. My own observations have led me to conclude that "the discipline of waiting" applies better in this case. Those words are deceivingly simple, yet they aptly describe one of the most difficult arts to master. Human nature and reflex action conspire to induce the angler to pull, even when the fish is nowhere near the fly; hence, the so-called "short take." Salmon frequently rise softly, which shows their mood and is characteristic in low water conditions.

When salmon are slow and deliberate in their approach, we have all been guilty of pulling up short. A solution to this problem, or at least a technique I try to practise, is this: once I've placed my cast, I follow a policy of deliberate distraction, focusing on anything but the drift of the fly. Foliage is excellent for this purpose. The procedure is to do nothing until contact has been made. In times of low water, the contact may be nothing more than a slight "tick" that many times has caught me off guard. The contact may or may not be accompanied by any sign of a rise, but usually there is a surface disturbance, however slight, or perhaps the sensation of stoppage as the current pushes against your line.

Knowing the lies that salmon frequent is invaluable. If you do not know the water, a guide who is local and experienced is indispensable. The object is to place the bug well above the lie, thus allowing it to drift toward the fish. If the fly begins to skim, drag has developed. It can be eliminated by mending, or drawing the line toward you and dropping the tip. Allow the cast to be fished out. Occasionally a salmon will leave the lie and take a bug that is hanging motionless below the angler. Never be in too much of a hurry to lift the line for the next cast. At times, slowly stripping the bug four or five feet can produce dramatic results. In depths of less than a foot, it's a bit unnerving to watch a large salmon arrow in on a bug from a dozen feet or more away and throw up a wall of water as it turns on the take.

The Cast

You might think that placing the bug slightly upstream will naturally cause a fair amount of false casting. However, there is a method which makes false casting unnecessary, while the angler moves downstream covering the water. There may be a technical name for this style of presentation, but if there is I'm not aware of it.

Bugging for salmon is not passive. Because of the weight of the rods and fly lines most commonly used in salmon angling, plus the extensive involvement of active upper arm, shoulder and torso and the rotation of the wrist that bugging requires, this method of casting is very active and requires constant attention. The technique of placing the bug up and across the current while moving downstream leaves little room for the purist's method of wrist flexing only.

I arrived at the technique by a process of trial and error. In 1985, I began fishing a particular run that had deep, fast-flowing water tight against the bank. I could wade out only about three feet before the stream bed dropped off abruptly. To complicate matters, the bank rose up sharply and was heavily interwoven with tangles of alders.

Because of the depth and heavy current, I hesitated to use chest waders. If I slipped into the deep water in my waders I could be in serious trouble — this is *not* my idea of tube rafting. Casting a wet fly in the traditional manner was all but impossible, and I removed flies from the branches over and over again. Roll casting was impractical in the swift current. But the run contained two lies. Since I could count on at least raising a fish almost any evening I was there, I decided that in spite of the frequent hangups, the lost flies and the occasional ruined fly line, returning and experimenting was worth the effort.

Gradually, I began to lift the line higher in order to avoid the hangups on my backcast. This strategy was not effective.

Gone Bugging

I then added to this higher backcast a revolving upper torso movement which allowed me to bring the line back, but in the corridor between the alders and the river. Having accomplished this, I swung the right-handed cast across to my left shoulder, continuing to move the rod upstream. My hangups decreased as I honed my skill. The one drawback of this method was that it sacrificed distance, but I found that presenting the bug above and alongside the fish to be the crucial factor in fishing a bug successfully.

The following instructions assume that you are right-handed, and that you are wading downstream in the river with the bank on your right.

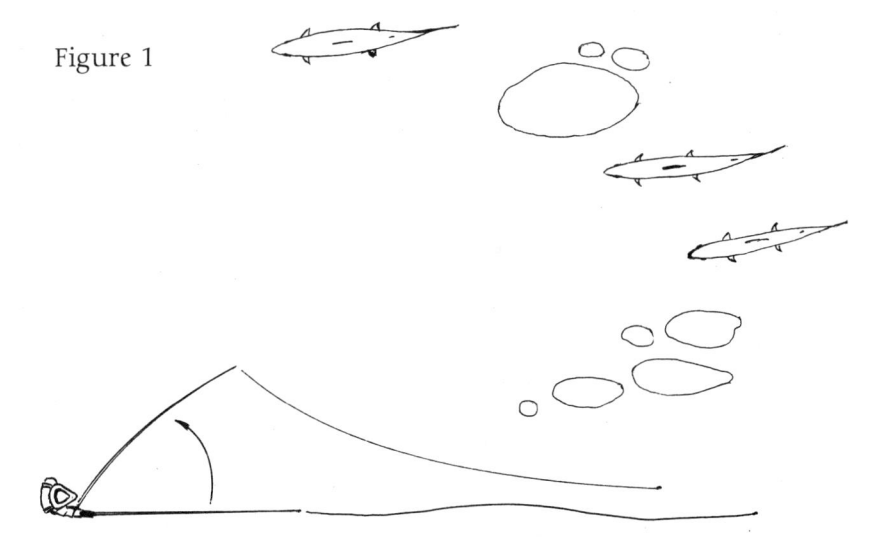

Figure 1

FIGURE 1: Beginning from a position where the spent cast hangs downstream below you, strip in the excess so that the remaining fly line will be sufficient to load the rod. The angler should be at a slight angle in relation to the line and the river flow. With the fly line in the left hand and the rod in the right, lift the fly line, orienting the direction to the left shoulder (not the right). You are now drawing the fly line up and over your head, swinging the line in an arc as you follow through.

Figure 2

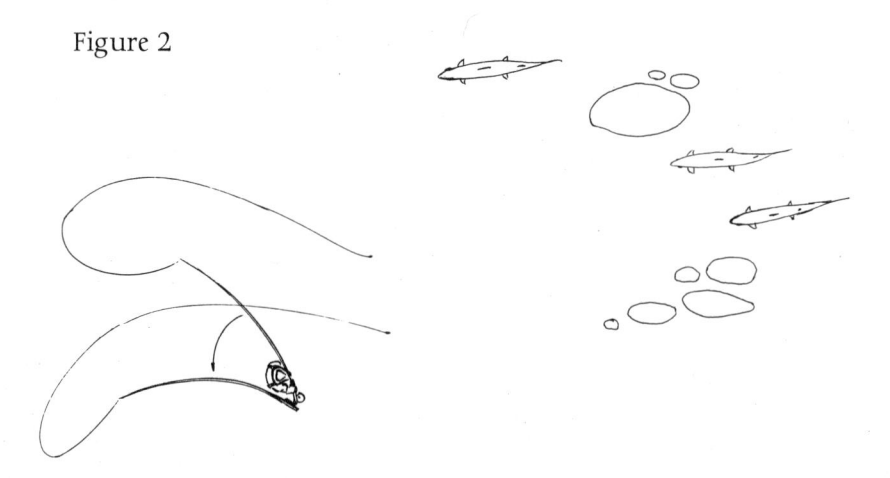

FIGURE 2: At the point where your right arm has lifted the rod to the area of your left shoulder, begin to create a circular motion, a crossover, as you continue to draw the rod up still higher, moving your arm now to the right. Behind you, the fly line is travelling in an elongated arc, elliptical in configuration.

Figure 3

FIGURE 3: With your right hand holding the rod at your right shoulder, continue to draw back to fully load the rod. The fly line is now travelling at its highest speed, all the while following an elliptical path, not behind you, as in the standard 45-degree wet fly cast, but to the side.

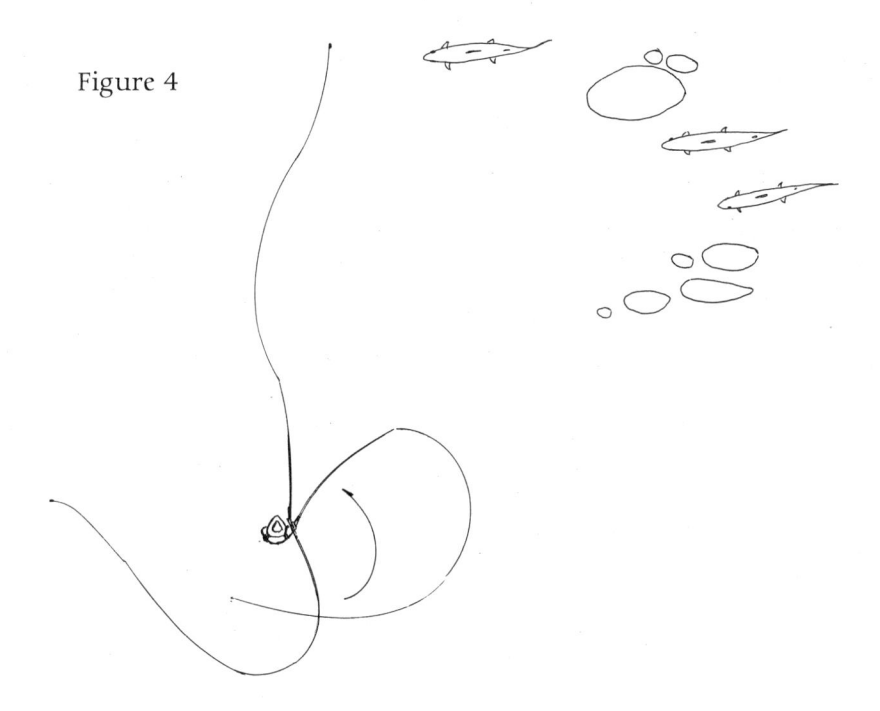

Figure 4

FIGURE 4: Now bring the rod forward, turning as you do to place the cast slightly upstream. Continue moving the rod upstream as the forward weight uncoils the running line. The fly should now be across and upstream from you, or nearly so, with the leader and the fly line following the drift of the bug.

In summary, the action is: up, over the left shoulder, to the right, and forward and out to the left. With practice you'll develop the style that is most comfortable for you. Remember that when you use this method of presenting your bug, you forsake distance for accuracy of placement. The object is to place the bug above and if possible broadside to the fish, without a lot of false casting.

The Water

Why are some anglers so successful in using the bug? Observations lead me to believe that while presentation of the pattern is important, so is the type of water over which a bug is fished. A friend uses bug patterns from the season's start to its end, and he is one of the most successful anglers on the St. John. By comparison, other anglers fishing the same waters with the same patterns have but limited success. You can tell if the angler is a bug fisherman. He knows what he is doing when he fishes known lies that seldom produce fish by traditional methods and with traditional patterns. These lies are for the most part in the tail sections of pools and runs, where the current speeds are slow.

After fighting through the shallow rapids, a salmon slips into a pool and finds comfort just above and behind some large boulders in the tail sections. Usually their first stopovers for a day or two are in places such as this. Other factors certainly come into play, such as water temperature and oxygen content. In the larger New Brunswick rivers, such lies are usually four to six feet deep.

These areas are very familiar to all anglers and are usually referred to as "slack water lies." They are fished over only occasionally, even though rolling fish are often evident. At times the upper portions of pools may be barren of holding fish, but not that slack water, although it can be maddening to fish because the lack of current speed frustrates standard tactics. Thus such water is usually ignored.

Salmon are surface oriented. Try to visualize for a moment what a salmon perceives in slack water. It observes a traditional wet fly hanging perpendicular as it approaches, because there is not sufficient current to let it ride on an even keel. Not infrequently a wet fly will snag among the rocks. The salmon may see another wet fly moving upstream in an erratic manner at a depth that may spark its interest. It sees a dry fly as a nondescript silhouette against a bright background, and under the right conditions it may rise to it more readily than to a wet fly.

A bug is in the salmon's element. It drifts in the subsurface of the current flow, and, because of its tendency towards neutral buoyancy, it rides horizontally. The fish sees it broadside when it has been fished on an upstream cast. Its submerged float looks natural, it enters the salmon's cone of vision from some distance upstream, and it approaches the salmon at the same speed as the current. I am convinced that the slow, deliberate, overhead approach of the presentation I have described induces the rise of fish in slack waters.

CHAPTER 5

A Way of Life

Many times I have been asked, "What was the St. John like before the dams were built at Tobique Narrows, Beechwood and Mactaquac?" I cannot answer that question, but I remember one very old angler who fished the St. John in the early 1980s. He passed away in 1984, the year that Fisheries and Oceans Canada imposed the grilse-only retention limit. In the years that I knew him, particularly 1979 and 1980, he commented that the fishing was almost as good as in the old days with relation to the number of large salmon that were hooked, even though the limit for the season was 15 salmon or grilse.

Fishing with him, I and many others shared in the experience of glimpsing the river as it must have been before the dams. We seemed to have stepped back into the past; the St. John for that brief time became once again a jewel in New Brunswick's crown of salmon waters, generous to all, veteran and novice alike.

Perhaps this story will convey the sense of nostalgia that we shared. It has less to do with bugs than it does with salmon fishing in general, for it mattered little then what fly one used because of the great numbers of salmon.

Bugging the Atlantic Salmon

My next door neighbour's son, John, had done some fly fishing for trout. The next logical step in his education was the Atlantic salmon. His interest perked up when I arrived home one day with a 16-pound fish, which I shared with his family.

One thing led to another as we chatted over a cup of coffee at the kitchen table. I told him that I would take him out if he got his licence, and that he shouldn't worry about equipment because I would lend him all he needed. After some instructions and a detailed lecture on the do's and don'ts of salmon fishing, we scheduled our trip for the next Sunday, June 22, 1980.

We arrived at the river before dawn and seated ourselves on the grassy bank, which was drenched with heavy dew. The smell of new growth hung thick in the humid air. From directly overhead came a loud, hoarse "SsquWARK!"

"Jesus! What the hell was that?"

I chuckled. "Just a heron, John, winging over to his feeding station on the bar."

Dawn soon broke, with overcast skies and a slight breeze blowing downriver. Other anglers were there, each waiting his turn to proceed down the run in order. I told John to step in ahead of me, telling him to pay close attention to those areas which I had pointed out as known salmon lies.

Handicapped by the unfamiliarity and weight of the rod, John did his best. I waded down to his position a number of times to help him select and tie on flies. He kept apologizing for the number he had lost and for banging the barbs off against the shelving bank of rock shingle. His low backcasts caused frequent hangups in the alders and did little to ease his discomfort. He was having a miserable time of it.

As the morning progressed, the overcast dissipated and the sun took the chill from the air. I raised one fish in the upper run at around seven o'clock, on a #6 Brown Fairy, but I could not get the fish back up, in spite of changing flies a number of times. By now, other anglers had landed six large salmon. John

A Way of Life

Hartt Island Pool, just below the Burpee Bar, Fredericton, New Brunswick, in about 1900. Note the anglers in their Sunday finery. PROVINCIAL ARCHIVES OF NEW BRUNSWICK P5/352.

was visibly discouraged. All six salmon had been taken in the run, in water over which we had previously fished. I told him that it was all part of the game. "You can't catch fish if your fly isn't in the water. The next cast, you could hook a twenty-pounder."

We had waded down to the lower end of the run. It was close to noon and time to head for home. John turned back to say that he had lost another fly. I waded over. He opened the small fly box. It was bare of the dozen or so flies I had given him except for a single #6 Black Bear Green Butt.

I told him that we would fish for about another half hour or so, then call it a day. I waded back upstream to my position, keeping an eye on John as he flailed away. Every once in a while I would offer encouragement, reminding him to shorten his line and keep his backcast up.

My eyes focused on the great blue heron stalking the shallow pools of the gravel bar. At that moment, as I stood there, rod underarm, fly line streaming in the shallows, I was more interested in the birdlife than in any fishing.

"I think I've got one."

John's shout snapped me out of my daydream. As he turned back to face me, I saw him holding his bowed rod with two hands. The scene did not immediately register. He must have snagged his fly on the rocks, and the current has pushed on the line, creating an illusion, I thought. I heard no sound from a protesting reel, saw no surface disturbance, nothing.

John stood looking puzzled. I was about to say something when a salmon exploded to my right, not five feet away as it tore past me. So that was it! The fish had clipped his fly and continued to move upstream. It did not react until the weight of the trailing fly line set the hook. Now the reel screamed as the fish angled into the current, hurling its mass into the main flow.

I yelled at John, "Keep your hands off the reel!"

Hurriedly reeling in my own line, I waded ashore, placed my rod in the fork of an alder, and ran, slipping down to where John still stood. After the initial run the fish had turned, moving downstream, ripping off line, backing in spasmodic jerks.

I got to John and told him, "Keep the tip up, we're going to land this fish. Just take it easy and do what I say."

"Okay, Mike," were the only two words he said for the next 20 minutes.

Reeling when he could and letting the fish run when it wanted, John fought a classic give-and-take battle that carried us some two hundred yards downstream from where the fish first took. John's neck and face became mottled with a lovely shade of red. He was concentrating hard, doggedly attempting to maintain his composure, but his emotions were on display.

A Way of Life

The salmon was tiring, yet it could not be lead into the shallows. I wanted John to beach the fish, but after it streaked into the current to renew the battle, I decided that the wisest course would be to wade out and tail it. The second time he got the fish to within leader length, I could see that the tippet was badly frayed. I told John to ease off the rod and I would try to guide the fish towards the tailer. What I was about to do was risky. As the salmon rolled weakly in the current, I had a sinking feeling that it would break off if it decided to make another run.

I waded out over my hips, catching my breath in the cold water. With one hand inching the leader towards me, the other extending the tailer, I offered up a little prayer. "Just a few more feet, just a few more feet."

"There," I said as the steel loop slid over the tail. With a gentle tug the snap ring locked into place. "I've got him, John!" I waded ashore with the salmon in tow, awkward with the weight of my bulging waders.

As I handed the tailer to John, I congratulated him on a job well done. For the first time, a smile brightened the serious set of his face. As he knelt beside the fish he began to mumble incoherently, and he babbled for the next minute or so, perhaps not quite believing the battle was all over.

The fish weighed 14 pounds. All depth, it had that characteristic bullet head typical of early run salmon. I examined the fish, noting that, in addition to a profusion of sea lice here and there, it had been scarred by nets.

I told John to look after his salmon and tag it. While cleaning his fish, he was amazed that a fly so bent out of shape could have held. Suddenly, he jumped back as an eel some three feet long came nosing up at the offal. I laughed at the look of pure disgust on his face as he backed away from the water's edge with the salmon.

"They're part of nature, John, they keep the river clean."

He looked at me aghast. "They may be part of the cleanup crew, but that son of a bitch is big enough to take my fish, and me with it!"

As he continued preparing his fish to take home, I felt a sense of deep satisfaction, knowing full well that another had joined the select fraternity of salmon anglers.

May 1, 1992. Scanning the St. John River earlier this morning, I noticed a pair of bald eagles winging upstream over the river, which is still clouded with melt water. The heavy spring floods of two weeks past have subsided and the water continues to drop each day. The buds of the swamp maples have been slow to swell. Spring is cold and late this year. The robins are back. As they search through the leaf litter for food, they are buffeted by occasional snow squalls that reach down the valley. It is difficult to think of the salmon season opening in little more than a month. In June there will be hatches of green drake and lead-wing mayflies, species which are extremely sensitive to pollution. Although the St. John River flows through the most heavily populated area in the province, it has, all things considered, excellent water quality, attested to by the presence of these particular insects as well as by the profusion of other life forms.

Where the Nashwaak enters the St. John River on the north side of Fredericton, anglers will soon be casting for striped bass. Even now the first run of bright salmon are entering the St. John.

A Way of Life

>-- >-- >--

Known locally as the Serpentine Run, this first run of bright salmon is named after a tributary which forms part of the Tobique River, a system that enters the St. John some hundred and fifty miles north of Fredericton at Perth-Andover, New Brunswick. It's inaccurate to call this the Serpentine Run, for that unique stock of Atlantic salmon no longer exists. In the 20-pound range, that fish began its migration in March under winter conditions, giving credence to the stories that the St. John had a fresh run of salmon every month of the year. (Even today some veteran anglers still swear that's gospel.) Migrating under the ice, these fish made their way upstream before the spring breakup. They arrived around May 15 at the confluence of the Tobique and Gulquac rivers, some two hundred and fifty miles from the Bay of Fundy. Then the fish stayed in the river system for a full year, to migrate to sea the following spring. In the 1920s, catches from camps such as the Gulquac Lodge were legendary.

Dr. George Frederick Clarke, of Woodstock, New Brunswick, wrote about the St. John in those days in books such as *Song of the Reel* and *Six Salmon Rivers and Another*. Clarkes's books are still well worth reading, if only to glimpse the river in its heyday and wonder, What if . . . ?

Although anglers still call the June salmon run the Serpentine Run, the real Serpentine Run is no more. As New Brunswick became more industrialized, the need for electricity grew, and hydroelectric development began in the valley of the St. John. One of the first dams on the river system was at Tobique Narrows. Built in 1952, it doomed the Serpentine Run to extinction; it is now thought that the fishways were inadequate. Successive dam construction over the years at Beechwood and Mactaquac, combined with clearcutting of the watersheds, pollution, poaching and overfishing, has reduced the great

Bugging the Atlantic Salmon

Nine-foot Atlantic sturgeon, Lower St. John River, Gagetown, New Brunswick.
PROVINCIAL ARCHIVES OF NEW BRUNSWICK P5/256.

salmon runs of the St. John and its tributaries to less than 5% of their historic size.

At the turn of the century, 100,000 salmon were commonly landed as part of the commercial catch in the harbour of Saint John. This huge catch, combined with catches from other Bay of Fundy rivers, made up the millions of pounds of salmon destined

A Way of Life

for export to the markets of New York and Boston. Every freehold adjacent the river strung gill and set nets to supplement the farm larder. Salmon were so common that the great fish was used for everything from an export commodity to fertilizer.

Today, a total annual run of 10,000 fish, of which 4000 are large salmon, is considered good. An exception was the great run of 1980, when some 10,000 large salmon and 17,000 grilse were recorded and trucked upriver to the release site above the Beechwood Dam. On opening day, I witnessed 52 salmon landed by 1:00 PM on the Burpeee Bar of the St. John River. Ranging in weight from 14 to 20 pounds, they were stacked like cordwood along the length of the bar. It was a sight to behold, with as many as four hooked salmon airborne at one time.

Despite the stress, the St. John boasts significant runs of shad, gasperaux and smelt, and the fabled striped bass are making a comeback. Some anglers fishing the lower pools will occasionally hook a 20-pound striper on the larger salmon flies they use in June. The river has a commercially viable population of Atlantic sturgeon, even though in much of their former range on the eastern seaboard they are rare to extinct because of pollution and overfishing. Some sturgeon are taken in the nets at Indian reserves, and fish in excess of 200 pounds are landed every year. Some are still reported that rival the giants netted by the early settlers to the valley.

There is now a large salmon hatchery at Kingsclear which helps to maintain the runs at somewhat acceptable levels. It attempts to offset the loss of the big spawners that are netted as part of the Indian food fishery. While netting by Indian bands is legal, most anglers believe it is destructive to the fish stocks. The Kingsclear Band has negotiated a creative resolution of conflicting rights: in return for giving up netting salmon, they have received help to establish the Kingsclear Lodge, on the beautiful Mactaquac Headpond, where they hope to exploit the Atlantic salmon sport fishing potential.

Salmon and Grilse Returns at Mactaquac Fish Hatchery

Year	Salmon	Grilse	Total	% Change
1967	1271	1181	2452	
1968	759	1265	2024	- 17.5%
1969	1750	2569	4319	113.5%
1970	2449	2968	5417	25.4%
1971	2276	2060	4336	- 20.0%
1972	5414	1030	6444	48.5%
1973	2842	3614	6456	.0%
1974	6682	7089	13771	113.5%
1975	8058	11060	19118	38.8%
1976	7134	14491	21625	13.1%
1977	9315	9684	18999	-12.1%
1978	4985	4140	9125	-52.0%
1979	2885	9755	12640	38.5%
1980	10451	17314	27765	119.7%
1981	3530	8353	11883	-57.2%
1982	2982	6223	9205	-22.5%
1983	2010	4843	6853	-25.6%
1984	7817	8657	16474	140.4%
1985	6961	7077	14038	-14.6%
1986	4143	7046	11189	-20.5%
1987	3435	8000	11435	2.2%

A Way of Life

Year	Salmon	Grilse	Total	% Change
1988	2600	9191	11791	3.1%
1989	4291	9587	13878	17.7%
1990	3919	7907	11826	-14.8%
1991	4226	7575	11801	.0%
1992	4203	7664	11867	.0%
1993	2980	3908	6888	-41.2%

FISHERIES AND OCEANS CANADA

Salmon migrating up the St. John River are trapped at the Mactaquac Dam and transported to the Federal government hatchery below the dam. After brood stock is selected, the remaining fish are trucked upriver to various release sites. Because of this, the St. John River fish can be counted and weighed, their physical condition noted, and a wealth of information gathered. With this data base, a very good picture has emerged that can apply to the whole Bay of Fundy region in general.

It used to be that, almost every year, the angling community was presented with the information that the salmon runs would be healthy, a prediction based upon statistical models applied to the St. John River. Invariably those runs failed to materialize. Fisheries biologists say that there is no reason why the St. John River cannot support a minimum annual run of at least 40,000 fish. Even so, ever since the 1980s, salmon stocks throughout the Bay of Fundy region have declined. Through the efforts of angling and conservation groups, commercial salmon fishing had largely been eliminated by 1985, and only Natives continue to exercise their treaty rights by netting of salmon for food.

Clearly other factors share the responsibility for declining salmon stocks. The consensus is that most smolt from Europe and North America migrate to winter feeding grounds off the Greenland coast. It was no coincidence that salmon stocks nosedived when a commercial fishery started up off that coast in the 1960s. Many rivers did not receive adequate fish to meet even minimum spawning requirements. Now, with an international agreement in place that severely limits the catch, that trend has been reversed. The Miramichi River is a good example of the success of these efforts; salmon stocks there show steady improvement year after year.

While the stocks in salmon rivers in the rest of Atlantic Canada have shown marked improvements in spite of problems created by netting, dams and pollution, for some reason the numbers of fish returning to the Bay of Fundy and New England rivers continue to be low. While no single factor can be blamed for this anomaly, it is surmised that a deficient food supply in the Bay of Fundy and Gulf of Maine has subjected migrating smolt, weakened because of lack of food, to higher mortality rates at sea than the smolt population as a whole. The incidental high seas catch of adult fish continues to be significant, too.

It is now believed that the Bay of Fundy and Gulf of Maine region has two distinct salmon stocks, one of the inner and one of the outer bay. Fish belonging to the outer bay stock come from the St. John, Magaguadavic, St. Croix and neighbouring rivers, as well as from the rivers of New England. This outer bay stock follows the general sea-wintering pattern, migrating to the Davis Strait area off the west coast of Greenland. Fish belonging to the inner bay stock, which come from the rivers in New Brunswick's and Nova Scotia's upper Bay of Fundy region, do not follow this sea-wintering pattern. Their offshore migration appears to be restricted to the continental shelf off Nova Scotia's south shore, as well as to the Bay of Fundy itself.

There are many unresolved mysteries about these inner bay stocks of salmon. I vividly remember the third week of April,

A Way of Life

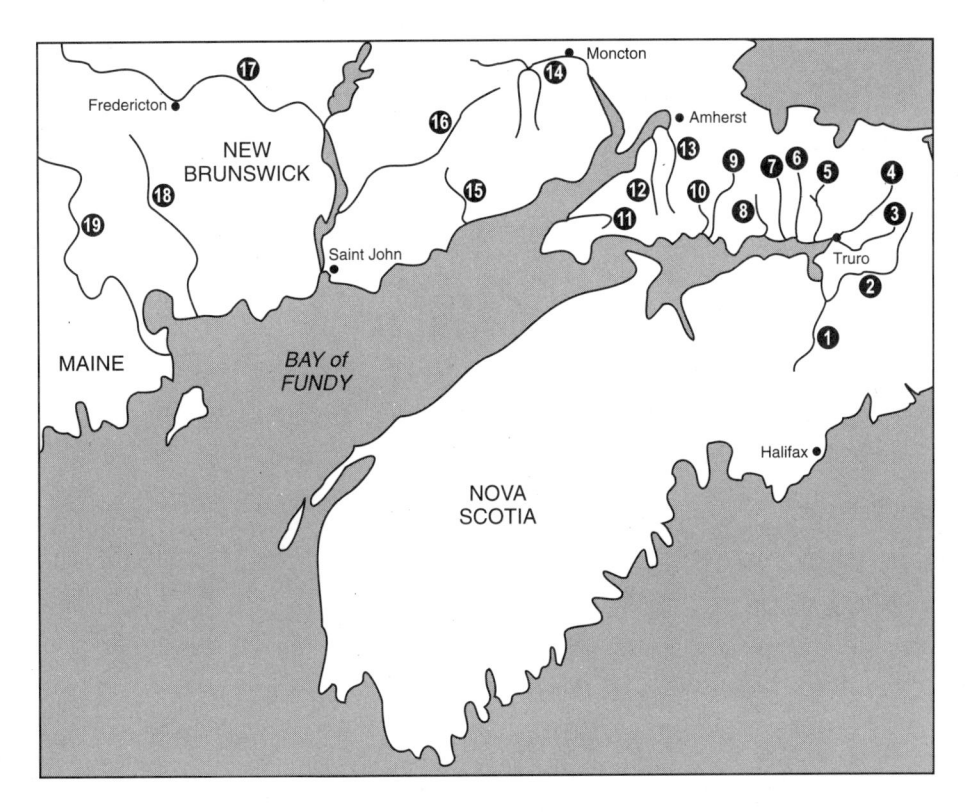

Major Salmon Rivers of the Bay of Fundy

- ❶ Shubenacadie River
- ❷ Stewiacke River
- ❸ Salmon River
- ❹ North River
- ❺ Debert River
- ❻ Folly River
- ❼ Great Village River
- ❽ Portapique River
- ❾ Economy River
- ❿ Five Islands River
- ⓫ Apple River
- ⓬ Hébert River
- ⓭ Maccan River
- ⓮ Petitcodiac River
- ⓯ Big Salmon River
- ⓰ Kennebecasis River
- ⓱ St. John River
- ⓲ Magaguadavic River
- ⓳ St. Croix River

Upper Bay of Fundy Rivers of Nova Scotia usually have their heavier runs in October.

Bugging the Atlantic Salmon

1972. I took my five-year-old nephew out trout fishing on the North River, Colchester County, which lies just on the outskirts of Truro, Nova Scotia. At Upham's Pool, using worms and spinners, we spent an hour hooking and releasing a number of salmon. In itself, this is not uncommon at this time of year. What was so startling was that not only were these fish bright, firm and full of fight, but they appeared to be spawning as well. Several of the salmon we released were dripping bright orange eggs, and one male of about eight pounds was oozing milt.

Over the years, I have questioned several fish biologists about this incident. Their responses have ranged from scepticism to mild curiosity. Some have suggested that those fish were actually steelhead trout, which do spawn in the winter and spring. But as far as I know there are no established sea-run populations of this species in Atlantic Canada. Supposedly Atlantic salmon do not spawn in the spring, yet I know what I observed.

Bringing the Atlantic salmon back to the Bay of Fundy rivers in the numbers that those rivers could support is a complex problem. We can only hope that the current low numbers represent the bottom of a cycle, and that nature will renew the resource if given the opportunity. Even so, the Burpee Bar on the St. John River remains one of the premier Atlantic salmon fishing spots in the world.

June 10, 1992, 3:30 AM. At this time of year there is light on the horizon, even though the sun will not be up over the hills for another two hours. Temperature: a cool 52 degrees, with a brisk breeze from downriver. Water: 2.98 metres, predicted to rise by 7:00 AM. Weather: clear and cloudless.

I arrive at the Burpee Bar on the St. John River at about 4:40 and string my rod. The breeze seems a little more brisk than I anticipated, and I should have worn a heavier sweater. Even though it's still dark, I hear purple martins warbling; somewhere behind me, a hermit thrush trills its descending scale of rapid flute-like notes. From Sugar Island, which is nothing more than a black silhouette, I hear the mournful "Wh-who-who-whooooo" of a pair of great horned owls drifting faintly across the river.

The top of the bar is quiet, the breeze putting a bit of a chop on the water. At this hour, if there are fish holding, you can usually spot them rolling. If they are moving, you can see their V-shaped wake as they slip up from the run.

I have the bar all to myself this morning. At 5:20 I select a #8 Green Machine. I put a short cast out. Just below the big rock I feel the "tick"; the rise was barely discernable. I let the bug be fished out, because sometimes if you don't react the fish will come back and take. I put another cast out, letting it drift over the fish. No reaction. Another pickup and another cast, a little further up. Just before the bug starts to angle, I get a glimpse — the tip of the tail submerging. No sensation of a pull or of the line stopping. Fish must have the bug. Gently lift the rod and feel weight. Nothing at first. Rod strain increases, and immediately the fish rips into the backing. Out she comes, three times, somersaulting. She changes direction, heading down the run. Two more jumps. Downriver 200 yards from where I started, I get the fish turned and wade out to tail her. The bug is set solidly in her jaw corner. I twist it out. As I release my grip, the fish lunges off with a resounding splash — a good spring salmon of about 16 pounds, all silver, fresh in, covered in sea lice. No length, so to speak, all depth and mass — she's a bullethead.

Bugging the Atlantic Salmon

I go down through the run, fishing a #8 Brown Fairy. No results. Past the point, I put the little bug back on. I feel a pull, but it's no salmon — I land an 18-inch sea trout weighing about three pounds. This is a surprise. There used to be a tremendous, predictable run of this species of brook trout during May and June, but the dams have changed everything. Now, in some years, no sea trout are reported, and in others, they are taken in fair numbers, some as large as six pounds. I'm happy with my three-pounder. The Green Machine has proved itself again.

May 10, 1994. I have been writing a good part of the winter. The spring has been exceptionally dry, contributing to the numerous forest fires in the province. I can only hope that we have some decent rains to keep the fires down and the water levels up. Nature's clock is working, as usual, and some large bright salmon have been reported on schedule in the Nashwaak. Today, I stopped in at a local fly shop to inquire about the reports. Yes, Wayne said, they were true, but the fish taken and released were not landed in the ordinary way. It seems that a number of fishermen have been trolling for striped bass at the mouth of the Nashwaak, just where it enters the St. John. Instead of bass, salmon have been walloping their lures.

Every year brings something new. One season, blue bugs were all the rage with the salmon. I wonder if they'll have a special colour preference this year.

Bibliography

Cummings, Bill. "Father Smith's Bomber." *Atlantic Salmon Journal* 39:4 (Winter 1990), 16-18.

Anderson, Gary. *Atlantic Salmon and The Fly Fisherman* (1985).

Clarke, George Frederick. *Six Salmon Rivers and Another* (1960).

Clarke, George Frederick. *Song of the Reel* (1963).

Flick, Art. *Master Fly and Tying Guide* (1972).

Hellekson, Terry. *Popular Fly Patterns* (1976).

Jorgesen, Poul. *Dressing Flies for Fresh and Saltwater* (1973).

Jorgesen, Poul. *Modern Fly Dressings for The Practical Angler* (1976).

Leonard, J.Edson. *The Essential Fly Tyer* (1976).

Schwiebert, Ernest. *Matching the Hatch* (1955).

Schwiebert, Ernest. *Nymphs* (1973).

Skues, George Edward MacKenzie. *Minor Tactics of the Chalk Stream* (1910).

Skues, George Edward MacKenzie. *Nymph Fishing for Chalkstream Trout* (1939).

Skues, George Edward MacKenzie. *The Way of a Trout With a Fly* (1921).

Stewart, W.C. *The Practical Angler* (1857).

Swisher, Doug, and Carl Richards. *Selective Trout* (1971).

Walker, Alf. *The Art and Craftsmanship of Fly Fishing* (1980).
Walker, Alf. *Mastering The Art of Tying Flies* (1976).
Wulff, Lee. *The Atlantic Salmon* (1958).

Index

A Apple River 97

B Bay of Fundy 91, 95, 96, 97, 98
Beechwood Dam 49, 85, 91, 93
Big Salmon River 18, 97
Black Bear Green Butt 87
Black Bug 57
Britain, British Isles (*see* United Kingdom)
Bomber 37, 39, 41, 42, 43, 50, 51, 64, 65, 66
Brown Fairy 22, 25, 29, 32, 86, 100
Buck Bug 43
Burpee Bar 26, 28, *30-31*, 68, 87, 98, 99

C Cains River 18
casting 78-82
Chapel Bar *26*
Cigar Butt 41
Clarke, George Frederick 91
Conrad 32
Cooper's Bug 39

D Debert River 47, 97
DeFeo, Charles 45
DeFeo Salmon Nymph 45
Devil Bug 39
Dobit 41, 42
Dungarvon River 18

E Economy River 47, 97
Electric Banana 57

F Fence Pool 20, 24
Five Island River 47, 97
Folly River 47, 97

G Glitter Bug 58
Glory Hole 33
Grand Cascapedia 39
Grand Pass 26
Great Village River 47, 97
Green Machine 29, 32-35, 52, 57, 99, 100
Green Machine Variant 57
Greenland 96
Griswold, F. Gray 39
Grub 40, *41*
Gulf of Maine 96
Gulquac 91
Gulquac Lodge 91

H Halford, Frederick 44
Hartland Salmon Pool *49*
Hartt Pool *26*, *68*
Hartt Island Pool 87
Hébert River 97
Henshall, James A. 38
Howland, Arthur 69
Humber River (NF) 72
Humpy 39

I Iceland 60
Ireland 60
Irresistible 39, 40

J Jacquet River 18
Johnny Bug 22

K Kedgwick River 19
Kennebecasis River 18, 97
Kingsclear Lodge 93

L Larry's Gulch 19
leaders 73
Leonard, Hiram Lewis 68
lines 72-73
Little Southwest Miramichi River 18

M Maccan River 47, 97
Mactaquac Dam 31, 85, 91, 95
Mactaquac Fish Hatchery 93, 94
Mactaquac Headpond 93
Magaguadavic River 18, 96, 97
Minas Basin 47
Miramichi River 41, 42, 45, 96
Moise River 72
Muddler Minnow *38*, 39
Musquodoboit River 41

N Nashwaak River 18, 23, 39, 42, 90, 100
Nepisiguit River 18
Northwest Miramichi River 18

Index

North River 47, 97, 98
nymphs 44-45, 48, *59*

P Patent method 37, 46
Petitcodiac River 18, 97
Phillippe, Samuel 68
Pine Ledge Rapids 64
Plain Brown 57
Portapique River 47, 97

R Rat Face McDougall 39
Rawlings, Marjorie Kinnan 38
Red Butt Buck Bug 19, 29
reels 72
Renous River 18
Restigouche River 18, 19-27, 46, 62-67, 72
rods *49*, 67-71
Rusty Rat 63

S Salmon River 18, 47, 97
Schwiebert, Ernest 44
Scotland 44
Serpentine Run 91
Sevogle River 18
Shubenacadie River 97
Skues, George E.M. 37, 44, 46, 47
Smith, Father Elmer 39, 42, 43
Smurf 59, 75
Snowball 58
St. Croix River 18, 96, 97

St. John River 17-19, 21, 26, 27-35, *49*, *68*, 72, 74-76, 82, 85-96, 92, 98-100
Standards 59
Stewart, W.C. 44
Stewiacke River 47, 97
Sugar Island *26*, 31, 99

T Tabusintac River 18
Tetagouche River 18
Thompson, Lewis 46
Thunder Creek 39
Tobique Narrows Dam 85, 91
Tobique River 18, 91

U United Kingdom 37, 45, 60
Upham's Pool 98
Upsalquitch River 18
Usk Grub 40

W water 82-83
Whiskers 42
Wood, Arthur H.E. 37, 45, 46, 47
Woolly Worm 40
Wulff, Lee 45

Z Zulu 40